YO-CQJ-122

Their Story:
20th Century Pentecostals

by Fred J. Foster

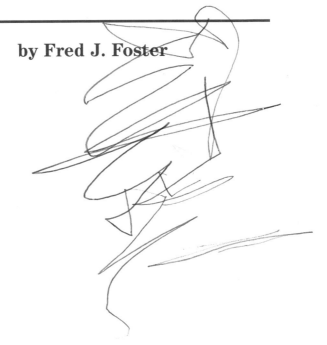

Their Story:
20th Century Pentecostals

by Fred J. Foster

©1965 Pentecostal Publishing House
entitled Think It Not Strange
Reprint History: Revised 1981, updated 1983, 1986, 1990, 1993, 1995,
    1998, 2003, 2004

Cover Design by Tim Agnew

All Scripture quotations in this book are from the King James Version of the
Bible unless otherwise identified.

Printed in the United States of America

Printed by

WORD AFLAME PRESS
8855 Dunn Road, Hazelwood, MO 63042
www.pentecostalpublishing.com

Library of Congress Cataloging-in-Publication Data

Foster, Fred J., 1929-
    Their story, 20th century Pentecostals.

    Rev. ed. of: Think it not strange. c1965.
    1. Pentecostal churches—History.   I. Foster, Fred J.,
1929-   . Think it not strange.   II. Title.
III. Title: Their story, twentieth century Pentecostals.
BX8762.A4F67 1986   289.9'4   86-26718
ISBN 0-912315-05-9

Foreword

For many years I have waited, watched and prayed for a book like this one.

After carefully reading the manuscript, I feel as though I have been treading on holy ground—ground made holy by those faithful men of God of the early days of Pentecost, who through vision, burden, tears, and consuming love for the full Apostolic truths, have been willing to withstand ridicule, persecution, and misunderstandings to bring this great Apostolic Church to this present hour.

Many of the things my good friend and brother, Fred Foster, has written about are familiar. Having been raised in the gospel work, and the son of a pioneering evangelist, I have both seen and heard these things.

The manner in which Fred Foster has written this book thrills my heart. The range and scope that this book covers makes it complete, and the straightforward manner of his presentation of the truth and facts that have been instrumental in bringing these truths to us is worthy of our sincere appreciation.

This book is beyond the ordinary, inasmuch as it is a book of our church history, a reference book and certainly one to give us a challenge to be Pentecost at any cost.

Since we are now in the third generation of the latter rain outpouring, it would be difficult to place a value upon these writings. Many of this generation are not acquainted with the way in which God has brought

His "People for His name's sake" out of tradition. Our young people need to know the truths presented here. This wealth of information can become a constant reminder to all of us that God loves this church, and has given us the marvelous revelation of "The Mighty God in Christ." This revelation caused our brethren in days gone by to, "Come out from among them. . ." and stand alone.

Several hundred years ago the wise man said, "But the path of the just is as the shining light, that shineth more and more unto the perfect day" (Proverbs 4:18).

James L. Kilgore
1965

Fred J. Foster

Author's Preface

This book is the fruit of a study which, in its beginning, was not intended to be a book. I became interested in the origin and experiences of twentieth century Oneness Pentecostals, and, to my utter disappointment, very little had been written or preserved of this illustrious past, and nothing from an organizational standpoint. I decided then to research this history, and in the early spring of 1963 the work was begun.

I am indebted to many people in the fulfilling of this work. Several of our old timers have retraced their steps for me, pulling from their memory golden gems of revelation to open the past to us who have wondered about it all. I deeply appreciate every individual who has contributed information of any substance.

I especially must give grateful credit to a few who went the extra mile.

From the beginning, upon discussing this with the General Superintendent of the United Pentecostal Church, Reverend Arthur T. Morgan, his words of encouragement and supplied material were invaluable. I am thankful for his magnanimous spirit toward me in this endeavor.

One of my fine instructors in Bible College, Reverend S. C. McClain from La Feria, Texas, was a tremendous source of inspiration through his letters of encouragement, and the supplied material. In addition, as a very generous gesture, he compiled several pages of notes from his own files and memory, since coming into the movement in 1912, and donated them to this work. I am overcome with gratitude.

Mrs. Jet Witherspoon, another one of my capable and long-remembered Bible College instructors, and the widow of the late former Assistant General Superintendent of the United Pentecostal Church, contributed much interesting material concerning her late husband's extensive work, and also about the many years she has been in this movement. Hearing from this noted woman added more fuel to the challenge.

Mrs. T. M. Bowen, a cherished Texas woman, who, along with her late husband, founded a great work in Houston, upon hearing of this work, began immediately to compile data which was very inspirational to me.

Reverend Oliver F. Fauss, a deeply-loved, longtime leader among us, who served as Assistant General Superintendent of the United Pentecostal Church, was a blessing to talk to and read after. I have quoted him on many occasions.

Reverend J. H. Gibson of Bryan, Texas, another appreciated old timer who was at the Elton, Louisiana Camp Meeting, made those days come alive to me.

Another contributor of substance was Reverend A. D. Gurley of Corinth, Mississippi. He worked in the organizational structure of this movement over the years, and was a member of the Foreign Missionary Board of the United Pentecostal Church.

Before his death, the beloved Reverend Howard A. Goss, former General Superintendent of the United Pentecostal Church, supplied vital information, even though very ill at the time. This demonstrates the spirit of the pioneers.

Reverend J. E. Dillon, the gifted and highly-respected former District Superintendent of the Texas District, gave me a large amount of inspiration in beginning this work.

I am the first to realize that this study is not all that it can be if the Lord tarries, but I am sure that it will call to remembrance many things to the readers who were contemporaries of the various phases of its history. When this happens, I would appreciate that one's writing me about those areas of history he knows about, with the thought that a new addition can be enlarged, and more light thrown on those interesting moments of the history of our movement.

From The Author

How times flies! Fifteen years ago this book was first published as *Think It Not Strange*, and I have been delighted with its reception. Reports from around the world tell of people reading it. Just this past Sunday, a Burmese Pentecostal leading pastor stood in our pulpit and told of reading the book several years ago in Northern India, and what it had meant to him. It has also been translated into Japanese.

Revival has continued among the Oneness people in these fifteen years.. Many thousands have been baptized in Jesus' Name and filled with the Holy Ghost in North America and around the world. The above pastor and leader started his ministry in his home country, Burma, seven years ago, and over 4,000 have received this experience. This has been repeated in many countries of the world.

I want to express appreciation to J. O. Wallace, manager of Pentecostal Publishing House, for his helpfulness in the revision of *Think It Not Strange* into *Their Story: 20th Century Pentecostals*. With updated material, new pictures, a new cover, and a new name, the same old beautiful story that deserves to be told, comes again with its impressive challenge, as we face the sunset of the 20th century.

Fred J. Foster 1980

Contents

Tables

"Stone's Folly," Topeka, Kansas, where the baptism of the Holy Ghost first fell in the twentieth century in the United States of America.

Chapter 1

Introduction

It was the great world-wide camp meeting in Los Angeles in 1913, with hundreds of preachers present from all over the Union and Canada. The occasion was a baptismal service in the pool near the big tent. Evangelist R. E. McAlister was speaking. He explained the different methods of baptism, versus the Scriptural mode. He mentioned the triune immersionist method— baptizing the candidate three times, face downward. He analyzed it thus: "They justify their method by saying that baptism is in the likeness of Christ's death, and make a point from the Scripture that Christ bowed His head and died." He concluded abruptly by saying, "that the Scriptural answer to all this was that the apostles invariably baptized their converts once in the name of Jesus Christ; that the words Father, Son and Holy Ghost were never used in Christian baptism."

An inaudible shudder swept the preachers on the platform and the people in the vast arena. The preacher noticed it, and stood in awesome silence. Brother Denny mounted the platform in one bound, took the preacher aside, and told him not to preach that doctrine or it would associate the camp with a Dr. Sykes who so baptized.

"Evangelist McAlister resumed his explanation, and said he did not mean to convey the idea that because the apostles baptized in the name of Jesus Christ, it was wrong to baptize according to the formula in Matthew 28:19. Thus ended the confusion on the platform. But the Gun Was Fired from that Platform Which Was Destined to Resound Throughout All Christendom, and that Within a Year."[1]

Little realizing that the sparks from his words would light great fires of revelation in the hearts of many of his hearers, R. E. McAlister walked from the platform that day fifty years ago. The sound is still ringing today.

When still a young man, it rang clear and strong in the author's heart, and his feeling is that much is owed this twentieth-century church. Through God, she has rescued, nourished and mothered us to the rich spiritual experience we enjoy so greatly. Countless thousands have been influenced by this religious awakening to bring believers into harmony with early church practices and beliefs. Very little is in print, though, about this awakening, and, in the light of this, I have embarked upon the journey of writing the history of the Oneness Movement.

REASONS WHY THIS HISTORY IS WRITTEN

(1) First of all, there is a definite need for such a history. The Oneness Movement has made a distinct mark upon the religious world and has shared a great part in the history of the Pentecostal movement of

the twentieth century.

(2) Many living today know very little of the struggles of the early part of the century. If this knowledge were better known, greater appreciation for the noble warriors of the past and for some still living in their elder life would be had.

(3) The world needs a history of the church in the twentieth century, so like the first-century church. The Bible is emphatic that Christ will come for a bride like unto the church He founded in the beginning of the church age; a church teaching and practicing the same basic doctrines the apostles propagated.

(4) History is filled with the attainments of those who were challenged to heroic deeds by the vision, accomplishment and devotion of men and groups of the past. May this history also accomplish this noble act in the lives of the ministry who read its pages.

THE PRIMARY CONCERN

The primary concern of this study will be the pinpointing of happenings and events relative to those Pentecostals who baptize by immersion in the name of Jesus Christ, and who receive the baptism of the Holy Ghost with the initial sign of speaking with other tongues, in relation to the second chapter of the Book of the Acts of the Apostles.

"Then Peter said unto them, Repent, and be baptized every one of you in the name of Jesus Christ for the remission of sins, and ye shall receive the gift of the Holy Ghost."[2]

"And when the day of Pentecost was fully come, they were all with one accord in one place. And suddenly there came a sound from heaven as of a rushing mighty wind, and it filled all the house where they were sitting. And there appeared unto them cloven tongues like as of fire, and it sat upon each of them. And they were all filled with the Holy Ghost, and began to speak with other tongues, as the Spirit gave them utterance."[3]

These Pentecostals also believe in the Oneness of the Godhead, rejecting the Trinitarian theory, and basing this doctrine on the biblical teaching that the Father, Son and Holy Spirit are manifestations of the one true God.

"And without controversy great is the mystery of godliness: God was manifest in the flesh, justified in the Spirit, seen of angels, preached unto the Gentiles, believed on in the world, received up into glory."[4]

THE ONENESS CHURCH GROUPS

In the past fifty years the Oneness message has had a tremendous growth. A recent report by the Associated Press in a national release stated that the United Pentecostal Church was one of the fastest growing church groups in the country. And so it has been the characteristic of these church groups to spread their message far and wide with great evangelistic fervor.

The groups who have played a prominent part in the Oneness emergence into the religious life of America are the following, in order of numerical strength: The United Pentecostal Church; Pentecostal Assemblies of the World; The Assemblies of Jesus

Christ; and The Church of the Lord Jesus Christ of the Apostolic Faith.

VARIOUS PENTECOSTAL CHURCH GROUPS

There are many Pentecostal organizations in the world adhering to various beliefs and forms of church authority. The one common principle where all are alike is the belief in the receiving of the Holy Spirit, as the early church did, with the initial evidence of speaking in other tongues. Most still cling tenaciously to the Trinity, but a select group has embraced the full scriptural truth of the Oneness of the Godhead and baptism in the name of Jesus.

The various church groups within the Pentecostal movement who have contributed somewhat to its present status are as follows, in the order of greater numerical strength: Assemblies of God; Church of God in Christ; United Pentecostal Church; Church of God; Pentecostal Church of God of America; International Church of the Foursquare Gospel; Pentecostal Assemblies of the World.; Pentecostal Holiness Church; Church of God of Prophecy; and Open Bible Standard Churches. There are several other smaller groups in different parts of the country and, of course, some stronger works in other countries of the world. All of these have contributed, to a certain extent, to the impact the Pentecostal movement has had on all the world. At this very time it is not uncommon to hear of preachers and laymen of the more staid denominational churches seeking for, and receiving, the baptism of the Holy Spirit.

TABLE I

CHURCH AND MEMBERSHIP GROWTH OF PENTECOSTAL BODIES

	1. 1936 churches–members		2. 1959 churches–members		3. 1979 churches–members	
Assemblies of God	2,611	148,043	8,088	505,552	9,291	939,912
United Pentecostal Church International	413	25,751	1,595	160,000	2,701	405,000
Pentecostal Assemblies of the World	87	5,713	600	50,000	—	—
Church of God (Cleveland, Tn.)	1,081	44,818	3,882	155,541	4,853	386,697
Church of God of Prophecy	—	—	1,214	35,526	1,791	30,000
Open Bible Standard Churches	—	—	265	25,000	280	100,000
Bible Way Church of our Lord Jesus Christ	—	—	—	—	300	131,753
Intl. Church of the Foursquare Gospel	205	16,147	697	79,012	823	—
Pentecostal Holiness Church	375	12,955	1,203	49,594	—	—
Pentecostal Church of God	81	4,296	900	103,500	1,100	135,000
Assemblies of the Lord Jesus Christ	—	—	—	—	—	—
Pentecostal Free-Will Baptist	—	—	—	—	125	3,000

1. U.S. Bureau of the Census, Religious Bodies: 1936
2. Yearbook of American Churches, 1960
3. The World Almanac and Book of Facts, Religions Information, 1980

THE MOVE OF GOD

There have been injected into the history of mankind, from time to time, weighty spiritual truths which, if followed, would be of tremendous blessing to the recipient. God has, through these revelations and happenings, led people into closer associations with Himself. It has always been the case, though, that the greater majority was too taken up in traditions of the past to follow God on to a fuller and deeper understanding of spiritual things and the heavenly will.

(1) First of all, God's standard was disobeyed in the Garden of Eden by the first parents.

(2) Who would believe Noah and the seemingly fantastic idea of the ark? Hindthought naturally shows us, in this instance, that God definitely was leading in a much more desirable way.

(3) When the children of Israel were in Egyptian bondage, Moses and his law appeared on the scene to lead them to the land flowing with milk and honey.

(4) While down in Babylonian captivity, God prepared a way of returning again.

(5) The long-awaited Messiah was then thrust upon the earth in the person of Jesus Christ.

(6) The Day of Pentecost, happening with all its spiritual significance, was next, where believers were baptized in the name of the Lord Jesus and received the gift of the Holy Ghost, with the accompanying sign of speaking in other tongues. Along with this were miracles, healings and a devoted life of holiness to the Lord.

(7) After a falling away from these early church-age truths, God raised up Martin Luther and the message

of "Justification by Faith." The Reformation was then to come to pass, led by such able reformers as Zwingli, Calvin, Servetus, Knox and Wesley.

(8) In the very early part of this century God again began pouring out the baptism of the Holy Spirit. This was bringing the church back to its original state.

(9) Then, in the middle teens of this century, light on the original baptismal formula and the Godhead was seen.

(10) Holiness standards were being sought out in compliance with God's Word. Surely the Lord was preparing a church for the last days.

The important thing to see is that in all these moves by the Lord, as He has revealed new truth or old truth forgotten or rejected, there were those ready to follow Him, no matter the cost. Whatever sacrifices they were called upon to make, or hardships which they had to suffer, some have carefully sought the will of God and followed Him all the way. They were ready to use the fire God had lighted in their own hearts to light other hearts, so that many could enjoy the blessings of this particular leading of the Lord.

It goes without saying that the vast majority of people would let God pass on by. Rejection of the moves of God has been the history of man and also his ruin.

Emerson said, "The greatest homage we can pay to truth is to use it."[5] This has been one of mankind's greatest failings because so much truth goes unused and unwanted. When truth comes marching by, too many let it march on without falling into step and following truth to its heaven-crowned destination. Stop-fard A. Brooke said, "If a thousand old beliefs were ruined in our march to truth, we must still march on."[6]

And because faithful soldiers have shouldered the responsibility of the truth of water baptism in the name of Jesus, the Oneness of the Godhead, and the baptism of the Holy Ghost, we venture into this, their history. It is a tribute to the memory of some already gone and others still living, those often-times over-looked champions of the cross, before whom this writer takes off his shoes and breathes the scriptural, surely this "is holy ground."[7]

[1]Frank J. Ewart, "The Phenomenon of Pentecost," p. 75-77.
[2]Acts 2:38
[3]Acts 2:1-4
[4]1 Timothy 3:16
[5]Tyron Edwards, "The New Dictionary of Thoughts" (Standard Book Company), p. 687.
[6]Ibid.
[7]Exodus 3:5

TABLE II*

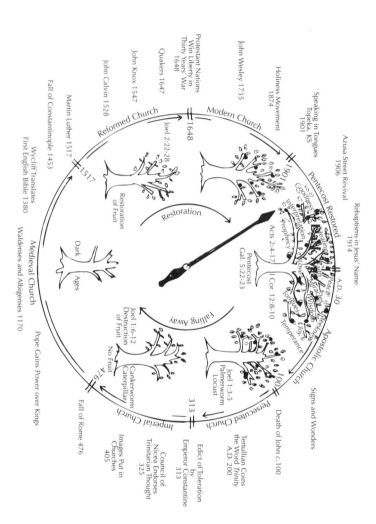

Rebaptisms in Jesus' Name 1914

Speaking in Tongues in Jesus' Name

Azusa Street Revival 1906

A.D. 30

Pentecost Restored

Apostolic Church

Signs and Wonders

Death of John c.100

Tertullian Coins the Word *Trinity* A.D. 200

Edict of Toleration by Emperor Constantine 313

Council of Nicea Endorses Trinitarian Thought 325

Images Put in Churches 405

Fall of Rome 476

Pope Gains Power over Kings

Waldenses and Albigenses 1170

First English Bible 1380

Wyclif Translates

Fall of Constantinople 1453

Martin Luther 1517

John Calvin 1528

John Knox 1547

Quakers 1647

Protestant Nations Win Liberty in Thirty Years' War 1648

John Wesley 1735

Holiness Movement 1874

Speaking in Tongues Topeka, KS 1901

Modern Church

Reformed Church

1648

Joel 2:22-28

Restoration of Fruit

Restoration

Dark Ages

Medieval Church

Falling Away

Joel 1:6-12 Destruction of Fruit

No Fruit

Cankerworm Caterpillar

Joel 1:3-5 Palmerworm Locust

313

476

Persecuted Church

Imperial Church

100

Pentecost Acts 2:4-17

I Cor. 12:8-10

Gal. 5:22-23

love, joy, peace, longsuffering, gentleness, goodness, faith, meekness, temperance, wisdom, knowledge, faith, healing, miracles, prophecy, discerning, tongues, interpretation

*S. C. McClain, "students Handbook of Facts in Church History."

Chapter 2

What Meaneth This?

Jerusalem was bustling at this particular time. People had thronged it from all over the civilized world, looking forward to this notable feast day. A strange phenomenon was taking place that day as had never happened before on any day of Pentecost. Thousands were pushing into the alleys and narrow streets around a building where the disciples of Jesus were staying. What was this strange thing going on? Were these actually drunk, as some were accusing? As people came closer and could see and hear, ". . .they were all amazed, and were in doubt, saying one to another, What meaneth this?"[1]

Countless questions such as this have been asked through the centuries concerning the manifestation of God's Spirit in the lives of believers as they respond to its workings. To understand what the Lord has been doing in this century we must journey back to the New Testament age as recorded in the Book of Acts. To better comprehend the Jesus' Name, Oneness teaching, and why the United Pentecostal Church is founded upon these beliefs, the history of the early church must be studied.

Any doctrinal concept must be based upon divine Scripture, that is, if the Bible is believed to be the only authoritative manuscript containing the Word of God, and this the United Pentecostal Church unquestionably stands for. It stands to reason, then, that the teachings of any church group today, to be correct, must harmonize with the teachings of the church of the New Testament.

These questions, then, come strongly to the mind searching for New Testament truth. What did they teach? What were their practices relative to baptism in water and the baptism of the Holy Ghost? Are there concrete, scriptural references to actual happenings in that early age? What did they believe about the Fatherhood of God, the Sonship, and the place of the Holy Spirit? These leading questions are answered very clearly in the Bible, and we shall deal briefly with them in this chapter.

THE EARLY CHURCH BAPTIZED
IN THE NAME OF JESUS

On that glorious day of Pentecost, described in part in the opening paragraph of this chapter, about 3,000 souls, hungrily searching for the way in which to be added to Christ's church, were advised by the apostle Peter and the eleven others, to be baptized in the name of Jesus Christ for the remission of sins. This is the first account in Scripture of the fulfilling of the commission Jesus had given before He ascended to glory.[2]

When the revival broke out in Samaria, following

the sign-confirming ministry of Philip, they were baptized with the same formula:[3] "Who, when they were come down, prayed for them, that they might receive the Holy Ghost: (For as yet he was fallen upon none of them: only they were baptized in the name of the Lord Jesus.)"[4]

Gentiles were also included in the Early Church revival. Cornelius was a Roman centurion who became extremely desirous of the blessings of God. The apostle Peter visited and preached to Cornelius and his household, and after they had all received the Holy Ghost he asked, "Can any man forbid water, that these should not be baptized, which have received the Holy Ghost as well as we? And he commanded them to be baptized in the name of the Lord."[5]

An enlightening thing is the apostle Paul's ministry. He very clearly outlined to us how he received the gospel: "But I certify you, brethren, that the gospel which was preached of me is not after man. For I neither received it of man, neither was I taught it, but by the revelation of Jesus Christ."[6] How will this apostle, who has not been taught of the others but only by revelation from Jesus Christ while in "Arabia,"[7] baptize? We follow him to Ephesus, where he is speaking to John the Baptist's baptized converts: ". . . John verily baptized with the baptism of repentance, saying unto the people, that they should believe on him which should come after him, that is, on Christ Jesus. When they heard this, they were baptized in the name of the Lord Jesus."[8] He not only baptized as the others but he believed in rebaptizing those who had not been baptized in the name of the Lord.

There is not found one place in the New Testament church where any convert was baptized in any way except in the name of the Lord.

THE EARLY CHURCH SPOKE
IN OTHER TONGUES

The strange phenomenon of speaking in a language never before learned was an intricate part of the first century church. The first account has been mentioned already, as a part of the basis in believing that speaking in tongues should be a part of the Christian experience.[9] One Pentecostal writer said ". . .try to visualize this tremendous spectacle of 120 simultaneously speaking in languages they had never learned. Foreign languages—(Weymouth); other kinds of tongues—(Rotherham); other languages—(Emphatic Diaglott). They were overpowered, influenced beyond control by the Holy Spirit, and suddenly became proficient linguists . . . This experience brought the religion of Christianity out of the realm of the theoretical into the experimental."[10]

Klaude Kendrick says, "The second of the Bible events concerns the ministry of Philip in the city of Samaria."[11] Though the account makes no mention of the tongues phenomenon,[12] Pentecostal writers go to considerable lengths to show that it was one of the mystical manifestations evidenced there. The third New Testament case, which is found in the ninth chapter of Acts, involves the apostle Paul. Here again actual reference to "tongues" is absent from the narrative, but[13] Pentecostal writers are convinced that Paul's experience included "speaking with tongues."[14]

The next account given in the Bible is when the Gentiles received the same experience as the Jews at Pentecost. The amazing thing about God is that He is no respector of persons.[15] Jew and Gentile, Greek or Barbarian, wise or unwise, all received the like experience. It was an extremely difficult thing for the Jews to understand, but here at Caesarea in a centurion's household, God broke down all barriers in receiving the gospel, so far as race is concerned. "While Peter yet spake these words, the Holy Ghost fell on all them which heard the word. And they of the circumcision which believed were astonished, as many as came with Peter, because that on the Gentiles also was poured out the gift of the Holy Ghost. For they heard them speak with tongues, and magnify God."[16]

Some twenty-five years later, under the ministry of the apostle Paul in the commercial city of Ephesus, a mighty manifestation was seen among the followers of John the Baptist. He asked them the pertinent question, "Have ye received the Holy Ghost since ye believed?"[17] They had not heard of such an experience, but after explanation, they accepted the teachings of the gospel and were baptized. When the apostle laid his hands upon them, the Holy Ghost came on them; they responding with speaking in tongues and prophesying.

In his first Epistle to the Corinthians, Paul devoted almost an entire chapter to the regulation of speaking in tongues. In this letter he thanked God he spoke with tongues more than any of them.[18] He also warned to forbid not to speak with tongues.[19]

To be a Christian in the early church was to have this thrilling experience with the Lord Jesus.

THE EARLY CHURCH ACKNOWLEDGED
JESUS CHRIST AS THEIR GOD

When those important leaders of the first-century church, Peter, Philip and Paul, preached and practiced baptism in the name of the Lord Jesus, they were acknowledging their belief that this was the name of the Godhead. Jesus had said, "I am come in my Father's name, and ye receive me not: if another shall come in his own name, him ye will receive."[20] The angel of the Lord had brought this glorious name from heaven for this miraculous child born to a virgin.[21] Jesus had also told them to baptize in the name of the Father, and of the Son, and of the Holy Ghost; and to fulfill this command they, knowing what this name was, baptized the early church in the name of Jesus.[22]

All Jews knew that the Old Testament Scripture taught there was only one God, that there was no God beside Him, and that He declared He knew of no other. God again declared that He was creator of all things, and also that it was He who distributed light and darkness. In addition, He said that unto Him every knee shall bow, and every tongue shall swear. They knew He proclaimed Himself to be a just God and a Saviour, there being none beside Him.[23]

With this knowledge, the Jews knew that if anyone suddenly appeared with these characteristics it had to be the Lord of the Old Covenant, because there was no other. There were no equal or lesser important deities or persons, because He had said that

His glory would not be given to another.[24]

So when Jesus Christ appeared on the scene of history, He told Philip and the others with him, "He that hath seen me hath seen the Father; and how sayest thou then, Shew us the Father? Believest thou not that I am in the Father, and the Father in me? the words that I speak unto you I speak not of myself: but the Father that dwelleth in me, he doeth the works."[25] This is why the apostle Paul, writing to the Corinthians, said, "To wit, that God was in Christ, reconciling the world unto himself."[26] Again, for the same reason, the Gospel writer John said, "In the beginning was the Word, and the Word was with God, and the Word was God . . . And the Word was made flesh, and dwelt among us, (and we beheld his glory, the glory as of the only begotten of the Father,) full of grace and truth."[27] And again, as was mentioned in chapter one, Paul said, "God was manifest in the flesh . . . preached unto the Gentiles. . . ."[28]

Now notice that all the things God declared about Himself in our second paragraph, the New Testament says belongs to Jesus Christ. He is called God by Thomas;[29] John and Paul attribute creation to Him;[30] Paul wrote, ". . . that at the name of Jesus every knee should bow, . . . and that every tongue should confess that Jesus Christ is Lord, to the glory of God the Father."[31] To the young preacher Titus was written, "Looking for that blessed hope, and the glorious appearing of the great God and our Saviour Jesus Christ."[32]

This study of deity, along with much other Scripture, leads us naturally to several conclusions about the beliefs of the early Christians:

(1) The God of the Old Testament and Christ of the New are one and the same person, and not two separate and distinct persons. That is why Paul wrote of Christ, "For in him dwelleth all the fulness of the Godhead bodily. And ye are complete in him, which is the head of all principality and power."[33] Jesus himself said, "I and my Father are one."[34]

(2) Jesus said, "God is a Spirit: and they that worship him must worship him in spirit and in truth."[35] Paul said, "There is . . . one Spirit."[36] So a logical deduction tells us that the Father and the Holy Spirit are one and the same.

(3) When the decision was made for the condescension, God veiled Himself in human flesh, born of the virgin Mary. In so doing, He became a God-man, with the flesh being the Son of God which housed God the Father within. This was the final theophany of God, for Jesus is the visible image of the invisible God.[37] We see the invisible God as we behold Him reflected through the Lord Jesus Christ.

(4) There is one God who has manifested Himself in three ways: Father in creation, Son in His redemptive plan, and Holy Spirit in His dealings with humanity.

(5) Let us conclude by saying that the doctrine of the Trinity is never mentioned in Scripture, neither are the terms God the Son and God the Holy Spirit. It is illogical to believe in the Trinitarian view, for even foremost theologians of that school of thought ask: "How could it be otherwise than difficult of comprehension?"[38] Another says, "It is a deep mystery that

cannot be fathomed by the finite mind, but must be believed, even though it cannot be thoroughly understood."[39] Again another says, "It is very difficult to understand and is an intellectual puzzle."[40]

The Early Church hinted at nothing like the teaching of the Trinity, but simply believed that Jesus Christ was God manifest in the flesh, and that He was God, not because a second person in the Godhead came to earth, but because God the Father, the only God in existence, came to earth, and was in Christ, reconciling the world unto Himself.

PENTECOST THROUGH THE AGES

It would be well in a dissertation such as this to remark somewhat about the intervening years between the first and the twentieth centuries. Much history has been written about the prominent church of the centuries, the Roman Catholic Church, but very little has been said about the heretics and resistance movements of the same period. It is interesting, yet extremely pathetic, to note that very little is known about these groups of people. Suppressed, ostracized and persecuted greatly, the things they stood for have been, as a whole, conveniently "misplaced," so far as history is concerned. As E. G. Moyer has already said, it is indeed strange that much of the records of so-called false teachings cannot be produced.[41] It seems logical to believe that, with so much controversy between the accepted church and its opponents, there would be much more written on the doctrinal views of the heretics. Only one conclusion can be drawn, and that leads us to believe that the church which kept the Bible a closed book also kept the beliefs of its opponents suppressed, so far as possible.

J. L. Hurlbut has said, "With regard to these sects and so-called heresies, one difficulty in understanding them arises from the fact that . . . their own writings have perished: and we are dependent for our views upon those who wrote against them, and were undoubtedly prejudiced. Suppose, for example, that the Methodist as a denomination had passed out of existence with all their literature; and a thousand years afterward, scholars, should attempt to ascertain their teachings out of books and pamphlets written against John Wesley in the eighteenth century, what wrong conclusions would be reached, and what a distorted portrait of Methodism would be presented."[42]

It is not to be understood, though the feeling exists, that all heretics stood for biblical truth. On the contrary, probably much was false teaching. But rays of light, whereby we can catch glimpses through the ages, let us know that many so-called heretics were actually children of God, standing for Bible truths and experiences they were willing to die for.

Let us now endeavor to catch a glimpse of some happenings akin to the teachings and practices of the New Testament church which will be of great interest to this history.

(1) **Water Baptism in the Name of the Lord.** It was said, "The formula of baptism, in the name of the Father, Son and Holy Ghost, which is cited as the traditional one by Justin Martyr, is perhaps not the oldest; but the older is perhaps the shorter formula which refers to Christ."[43] Williston Walker says, "This

appears in the Trinitarian baptismal formula, which was displacing the older baptism in the name of Christ."[44] Mention is made throughout history of some who baptized in the name of Christ as late as the eighth century, although they were branded as heretics and died for the truth they boldly upheld."[45]

It is distinctly seen that these noted authors and compilers of history, not looking through the eyes of a biased theologian, readily agree that the apostolic formula in baptism was "the name of Jesus." Sad as it is that very little of the teachings of the "heretics" has been preserved, it is gratifying that these references above have spoken on this tremendous subject. It is noticeable, though, that the later editions of some encyclopedias are dropping the references to the Jesus' name formula in baptism. It causes one to wonder if a modern suppression of truth concerning the practices of the early church is now going on.

(2) **The Oneness of God.** H. G. Wells, speaking of the third and fourth centuries, said, "The chief views that the historian notices are those of the Arians, the Sabellians, and the Trinitarians. The Arians taught that Christ was less than God. The Sabellians taught that he was a mode or aspect of God—God was Creator, Saviour and Comforter, just as one man may be father, trustee and guest; the Trinitarians, of whom Athanasius was the great leader, taught that the Father, the Son and the Holy Ghost were three distinct Persons, but one God. The latter mystery seems to the writer, he must confess, a disastrous ebullition of the human mind entirely inconsistent with the plain account of Jesus preserved for us in the Gospel."[46]

The teaching of the Oneness of God has pervaded the centuries, as has been written by theologians in an endeavor to refute it. "Other writers, laying stress on the unity of God, seemed in danger of forgetting the distinction of persons. This error is commonly known as Sabellianism, from Bishop Sabellius who taught that Father, Son and Holy Spirit are simply three aspects or manifestations of God. This error has appeared many times in the history of the church and is current today."[47]

(3) **Speaking in Tongues**. The speaking in tongues phenomenon has also been in existence in almost any age. Irenaeus, Tertullian, Justin Martyr, Origen, and Augustine all wrote of this strange happening in their particular era. Two groups, the Albigenses and the Waldenses, grew to prominence in France during the latter part of the twelfth century. "Both groups repudiated much of the accepted Roman Catholic doctrine. They believed and practiced the Spirit-filled life, with speaking in tongues being one of their outstanding characteristics."[48] In the year 1208, Pope Innocent III had the Albigenses completely slaughtered. Many Catholics were also killed in making sure all Albigenses were extirpated.

A great number of the Waldensians escaped a similar fate by fleeing into the valleys of northern Italy, where they survived several centuries of persecution. In 1458, they merged with the Moravians, another Spirit-filled people.

(4) **Revival in Wales**. Quoting F. N. Peloubet, who said, "A revival in Wales in the late nineteenth century caused the Yorkshire Post to say: 'Young Welshmen

and women who know little or no Welsh . . . now under the influence of revival, voluntarily take part in public prayer—but the language employed is almost invariably not the familiar English, but the unknown, or supposed to be unknown, Welsh biblical phrases which they never used before.'"[49]

(5) **Girl's School in India**. Quoting the same source: "Mr. William T. Ellis, a newspaperman, wrote regarding a visit to India, where Pandita Ramabai had a well-known school for girls: 'I have stumbled upon an extraordinary religious manifestation . . . I shall simply narrate, soberly and consecutively, what I have seen and heard concerning this baptism with fire and pouring out of the gift of tongues, whereby ignorant Hindu girls speak in Sanskrit, Hebrew, Greek, English, and other languages as yet unidentified.'"

Many others received the baptism of the Holy Ghost with the initial sign of speaking in tongues in the nineteenth century. Because it was an uncommon happening, and there was no theological emphasis upon it, they did not know exactly what they had received, only that it was a thrilling experience.

After the turn of the century, when God began pouring out His Spirit around the world in a mighty "end-day" deluge, and it was seen in the light of biblical truth that speaking in tongues accompanied the Holy Ghost baptism of the New Testament church, it was found that many had been receiving a like experience for several years.

"V. P. Simmons of Frostproof, Florida wrote a tract in which he told of many gracious manifestations of the Spirit that he had seen in New England.

He stated, 'In 1854, Elder Edwin Burnham interpreted the same. The writer knew both of these men of God well, and had often sat under their preaching. They were large men physically, mentally and spiritually.' He witnessed a revival in New England in 1873, and stated: 'The talking in tongues, accompanied largely with the gift of healing, was manifested.'"[50]

In the year 1873, Dwight L. Moody and Ira Sankey went to England. The story of their visit is recorded in a book entitled, "Moody and Sankey in Great Britain," by Robert Bayd, published in 1875.

"The two workers from America did not receive a very good reception at the beginning. They were invited to Sunderland, but their presence there aroused a good deal of opposition from unsympathetic ministers. A delegation of young men waited on Mr. Moody and asked him to speak at the Y.M.C.A. He consented, and the Lord began to send a gracious awakening. Mr. Bayd described what he himself witnessed at one meeting. 'When I got to the rooms of the Y.M.C.A. I found the meeting on fire. The young men were speaking in tongues and prophesying. What did it mean? Only that Moody had been addressing them. Many of the clergy were so opposed to the movement that they turned their backs upon our poor innocent Y.M.C.A. for the part we took in the work.' The same story was also published in 1876 by the American Publishing Company, Hartford."

Mary Woodworth Etter, who became a powerful evangelist in the fledgling Pentecostal movement, in telling of her earlier ministry which began in 1876 in the United Brethren Church, said: "Almost from the beginning of my ministry some spoke in unknown languages, but I did not understand it, and as I was the only leader, I did not have much time to investigate and explain it; but I knew it was of God."[51]

There is much in the statement of Pascal, who said, "There are two peculiarities in the truths of religion: a divine beauty which renders them lovely, and a holy majesty which makes them venerable."[52] And so it has been with the particular truths we are discussing in this history; divinely beautiful and awesome, they have had their dedicated disciples.

Much more could be written on these thrilling subjects and of their pervading the centuries, but sufficient has been said to give a distinct idea of how biblical truth has been believed, practiced, and died for through the ages. May the winds of memory, blowing off the history of the past, drive some of the consecration and dedication of those courageous people into this latter half of the twentieth century.

[1]Acts 2:12
[2]Acts 2:37, 41
[3]Mark 16:20
[4]Acts 8:5, 15, 16
[5]Acts 10:47-48
[6]Galatians 1:11, 12
[7]Galatians 1:17
[8]Acts 19:4-5
[9]Acts 2:1-4
[10]F. J. Ewart, "Phenomenon of Pentecost," p. 14, 15.
[11]Klaude Kendrick, "The Promise Fulfilled" (Gospel Publishing House).
[12]Acts 8

[13]P. C. Nelson, "A Handbook of Pentecostal Theology, based on the Scriptures and following the lines of the Statement of Fundamental truths, as adopted by the General Council of the Assemblies of God."

[14]Carl Brumback, "What Meaneth This? A Pentecostal Answer to a Pentecostal Question."

[15]Acts 10:3-4

[16]Acts 10:44-46

[17]Acts 19:1-6

[18]I Corinthians 14:18

[19]I Corinthians 14:39

[20]John 5:43

[21]Matthew 1:21

[22]Matthew 28:19; Acts 2:38

[23]Isaiah 45

[24]Isaiah 42:8

[25]John 14:9-10

[26]II Corinthians 5:19

[27]John 1:1-14

[28]I Timothy 3:16

[29]John 20:28

[30]John 1:3, 10; Colossians 1:16; Hebrews 1:2

[31]Philippians 2:10

[32]Titus 2:13

[33]Colossians 2:9

[34]John 10:30

[35]John 4:24

[36]Ephesians 4:4; I Corinthians 12:13

[37]Colossians 1:15

[38]Myer Pearlman, "Knowing the Doctrines of the Bible," p. 69.

[39]William Evans, "The Great Doctrines of the Bible," p. 27

[40]Addison H. Leitch, "Interpreting Basic Theology," p. 22-24.

[41]E. G. Moyer, "Truths on Water Baptism," p. 26.

[42]Jesse Lymen Hurlbut, "The Story of the Christian Church," p. 66.

[43]Neanders, "History of the Christian Church," p. 16 (McClain).

[44]Williston Walker, "A History of the Christian Church," p. 58.

[45]S. C. McClain, "Students Handbook of Facts in Church History," p. 29.

[46]H. G. Wells, "The Outline of History," p. 545.

[47]Pearlman, "Knowing the Doctrines of the Bible," p. 70.

[48]S. C. McClain, "Students Handbook of Facts in Church History,"

p. 42, 43; J. L. Hurlbut, "The Story of the Christian Church," p. 141, 142.

[49]"Peloubet's Bible Dictionary," p. 704.
[50]Stanley H. Frodsham, "With Signs Following," p. 9, 10.
[51]Carl Brumback, "Suddenly From Heaven," p. 13.
[52]Frezon Edwards, "The New Dictionary of Thoughts," p. 689.

The Azusa Street Mission, Los Angeles, California.

Chapter 3

The Early Years of the Latter-Day Outpouring

THE TOPEKA OUTPOURING

A remarkable happening in a small Bible School in Topeka, Kansas on January 1, 1901 is credited to be the lighting of the fire that has swept the world with the Pentecostal experience in this century. This school has been called "the birthplace of the most startling religious phenomenon of modern times."[1]

Little did Charles F. Parham realize the great significance his desires for the Lord's work would bring on the twentieth century. Ambitious as he was to further the cause of Christ, his fondest dream could not have enveloped all the glory God would bring on the earth because of the spiritual hunger in his and the students' hearts.

In 1898, twenty-five-year-old Charles F. Parham and his twenty-one-year-old wife of two years established the Bethel Divine Healing Home in Topeka, Kansas. "The purpose of the Bethel Home was to provide home-like comforts for those who were seeking healing, while we prayed for their spiritual needs, as well as for their bodies. Christian homes for orphan children, and work for the unemployed was also founded. Special studies were given to ministers and evangelists, and many workers were instructed in Bible truths and trained for the gospel work."[2]

At this time Parham also edited a paper, *The Apostolic Faith*, published twice a month. "At first we had a subscription price; later we announced, 'For subscription price see Isaiah 55:1,' and the Lord wonderfully provided. The paper was filled with wonderful testimonies to healing and sermons containing teachings of the Home."[3]

During this period of church history there was great unrest. The larger denominations had lost much of their spiritual steam, creating a tremendous hunger in the hearts of many desiring spiritual strength that could not be obtained in the more formal worship services. New groups sprang up with various names and doctrines, but most of their founding was predicated on the hunger in their hearts for reality in religious experience.

Parham was one of these, and growing more intent he made a momentous decision: "Our hearts were stirred to deepen our consecration and to search the Word. Deciding to know more fully the latest truths restored by latter-day movements, I left my work in charge of two Holiness preachers and visited various movements . . . in Chicago . . . Cleveland . . . Nyack, New York . . . Shiloah, Maine and many others.

"I returned home fully convinced that while many had obtained real experiences in sanctification and the anointing that abideth, there still remained a great outpouring of power for the Christians who were to close this age."[4]

Parham wrote on: "I went to my room to fast and pray, to be alone with God, that I might know His will for my future work. Many of my friends desired me to open a Bible school. By a series of wonderful miracles we were enabled to secure what was then known as Stone's Folly, a great mansion patterned after an English castle, one mile west of Washburn College in Topeka."[5]

Stone's Folly was a beautiful, elaborate building which was never finished as the builder anticipated because of lack of funds. The stairway of beautifully carved cedar, cherry wood and bird's-eye maple stopped with the second floor, and the third floor had to be finished with much cheaper materials of pine and common maple. The extraordinary two-domed mansion had a cupola at the back, and also an observatory tower, reached by winding stairs. This three-story, thirty-room mansion is where God would signal the latter-day outpouring of the Holy Ghost.[6]

A Topeka newspaper, in an article about Parham's school, said: "The discovery of a new religion, or perhaps, as its devotees claim, the recovery of that which was lost, has been made in Kansas, of course. The Rev. Charles Parham claims to be the discoverer, and has established a school where the new faith is practiced. It is called Bethel Gospel School and is located at Stone's Folly near Topeka. Forty enthusiasts are following Parham in his new faith. They pray for what they get, and get what they pray for. They do no work, yet they have plenty to eat and wear. They say the Lord provides. The school was established last September. (Rev. Parham says the school was founded in October).[7] Parham declares that on New Year's Day one of the students, a Miss Ozman, became suddenly gifted with a strange tongue, spoke in a language unknown to herself or the others and knew not what she said. 'The next day,' said Parham, 'I went down town, and, upon my return, found all the students sitting on the floor talking in unknown tongues, no two talking the same language, and no one understanding his or her neighbor's speech. From that time on, the spiritual development was marvelous.'[8]

The account in the paper is very interesting, but the events leading up to this mighty outpouring are very impressive also. After beginning classes in his school, their studies hit a snag. "What about the second chapter of Acts?"[9] This was the problem Parham had wrestled with for sometime. Having to be gone from the school for three days of services, he describes his feelings and what he told the students thus: "I believed our experience should tally exactly with the Bible, and neither sanctification nor the anointing that abideth taught by Stephen Merritt and others tallied with the second chapter of Acts. Having heard so many different religious bodies claim different proofs as the evidence of their having the Pentecostal baptism, I set the students at work studying out diligently what was the Bible evidence of the baptism of the Holy Ghost, that we might go before the world with something that was indisputable because it tallied absolutely with the Word."[10]

When Parham returned he was anxious to be with the students and hear what they had found concerning the biblical problem he had left with them. Eagerly he rang the bell about 10:00 o'clock on the morning he arrived, calling the students into the chapel. As he questioned them one by one, to his astonishment they all had the same story: "that while there were different things which occurred when the Pentecostal blessing fell, the indisputable proof on each occasion was that they spoke with other tongues."[11]

Lilian Thistlethwaite in her account of subsequent events said: "Services were held daily and each night . . . All felt the influence of a mighty presence in our midst. The service on New Year's night was especially spiritual and each heart was filled with hunger for the will of God to be done in them. One of the students (Agnes N. Ozman, Later LaBerge) . . . asked Mr. Parham to lay hands upon her that she might receive the Holy Spirit. As he prayed, her face lighted up with the glory of God and she began to speak with other tongues. She afterward told us she had received a few words while in the Prayer Tower (this was the observatory tower which was used for a continuous prayer meeting at this time), but now her English was taken from her, and with floods of joy and laughter she praised God in other languages."[12]

This happened New Year's Day, 1901, and on the third, Parham and many others likewise received the same experience. Also in the school were twelve ministers of different faiths who were filled with the Holy Spirit and spoke with tongues.

"No sooner was this miraculous restoration of Pentecostal power noised abroad than we were besieged with reporters from Topeka papers. Kansas City, St. Louis and many other cities sent reporters, who brought with them professors of languages, foreigners, government interpreters, and they gave the work the most crucial test. One government interpreter claimed to have heard twenty Chinese dialects distinctly spoken in one night. All agreed that the students were speaking in languages of the world, and that with proper accent and intonation."[13]

THE SIGNIFICANCE
OF THE TOPEKA OUTPOURING

The unusual significance concerning the Topeka outpouring is not that it was the first time in the modern age people had spoken in tongues, but that it was the first known experience of people's seeking for the baptism of the Holy Ghost with the expectation of speaking in tongues. "From this time Pentecostal believers were to teach that the baptism of the Holy Spirit should be sought, and that it would be received with the evidence of tongues. For this reason the experience of Agnes Ozman is designated as the beginning of the modern Pentecostal revival."[14]

The practices and teachings of the early church were again being brought into effect by the moving of God's Spirit. Many believed this was God's time to again restore to the church all that the New Testament church had, and by the grace of God, they were willing to stake everything on it.

THE FIRE SPREADS

Parham and workers from the school held several revivals in different cities of the area. While this group was away from the school, the ones left prayed long hours for the success of the meetings.

News of this phenomenon spread far and wide and crowds of people would be on hand to hear the evangelist speak.

"The fire quickly spread to Kansas City, Lawrence, Galena, Melrose, Keelville and Baxter Springs. When the fire would reach a city or town, Brother Parham and his workers would hold a revival meeting. Sometimes, as at Galena and Baxter Springs, no building could hold the crowds, and they would pitch a tent in a convenient location and carry on for months . . .

"Soon after the revival in Topeka, ministers from various denominations began to inquire after this new way. Many of the more noble, who searched the Scriptures and found that the experience was scriptural, became seekers at the altars. Many were filled with the Holy Ghost, speaking with other tongues, and joined Brother Parham in his vigorous crusades."[15]

[1]Ewart, "Phenomenon of Pentecost," p. 30.
[2]Sarah E. Parham, "The Life of Charles F. Parham," p. 39.
[3]Ibid., p. 39.
[4]Ibid., p. 48.
[5]Ibid., p. 49.
[6]"Topeka Mail and Breeze," Feb. 23, 1901 (Kansas Historical Society).
[7]Ibid.
[8]Parham: "Parham," p. 51.
[9]Ibid., p. 51.
[10]Ibid., p. 52.
[11]Ibid.
[12]Ibid., p. 59.

[13]Ibid., p. 54, 55.
[14]Kendrick, "The Promise Fulfilled," p. 53.
[15]Ewart, "Phenomenon of Pentecost," p. 32.

Chapter 4

A Fire That Cannot be Extinguished

"Suddenly from heaven!" As it was at the beginning on the day of Pentecost, there was something about this phenomenal happening that could not be sidelined. It was destined to enlarge its borders, and so we shall see it, step by step, as it increased to its present stage.

GALENA, KANSAS REVIVAL

A notable meeting was started in the lead and zinc mining town of Galena, Kansas in the fall of 1903, and lasting on through the winter. God worked in a most unusual way, healing the sick and filling many with the Holy Spirit. The largest building in town, seating 1,000, could not take care of the crowds that swarmed to these meetings. The *St. Louis Globe Democrat* reported the meeting thus: "Galena, Kansas, January 1, 1904—The evangelistic meetings which have been held at this place by the Rev. Parham for the past six weeks celebrated the New Year by baptizing the converts in Spring River this afternoon.

"These meetings have been a success from the

beginning, and fully 500 have been converted. Some have already been immersed, but today's list counts 250. Many of the most prominent people in town have professed to having been healed of blindness, cancer, rheumatism and other diseases, and it has been such a spiritual revival as Galena has not experienced in years, if ever.

"The services were to have been closed last night with the all-night watch meeting, but the business men rallied and made good the expenses for another month's service."[1]

It was here at this time that Howard A. Goss, destined to be a prominent figure in Pentecost, was first introduced to the Pentecostal message.

Goss said, "This was my first contact with Pentecostal people or with Christianity of any sort, for that matter . . . Around the time the Galena meeting first started, . . . my high school teacher . . . spoke to me about serving the Lord. In all my life, this was the only time anyone had ever spoken to me about my soul. After I became fully convinced that infidelity was wrong, I went forward during the next meeting to the place of prayer, earnestly praying and seeking God.

". . . On one of the coldest days of the entire winter that followed, I remember Brother Parham baptizing around 100 converts in Spring River before a tremendous crowd assembled in the open. I was one of that hundred."[2]

TEXAS WAS NEXT

From Galena, Joplin and Baxter Springs, the revival fires spread. The next direction it went was Texas.

God uses strange situations to further His cause, and so it was with the story behind the Holy Ghost outpouring in Orchard, Texas.

T. Walter Oyler became very ill while farming at Orchard. He had come to Texas some years before from his native state of Missouri, and now decided to go back there to be among his relatives for his last days on this earth, but the Lord had other plans. He and his faithful wife heard of the glorious but strange revival in Galena, Kansas, and decided to go over and see for themselves. While there, as has often been the case in revival meetings, they could not resist the influences of the Holy Ghost, and they were soon thrillingly baptized with the Spirit.

Later in Missouri they attended Parham's important meeting at Joplin, and there Oyler was miraculously healed by the power of the Lord.[3] Gloriously healed and baptized with the Holy Ghost, he naturally wanted to go back to Orchard and spread the good tidings. In Joplin he and his wife met Mrs. Anna Hall, an appealing woman, whom they prevailed upon to accompany them back to Texas to hold a revival meeting. This she did, and began there on March 21, 1905.[4]

THE BIRTHPLACE
OF THE TEXAS OUTPOURING

With the booming revival which followed, Orchard, a little town on the prairie forty-five miles from Houston, became the birthplace of the outpouring of the Holy Ghost in Texas. Parham wrote, "There were only five or six Christians here, but in two weeks there were only about that many sinners. In the whole section, from far and near, they come and are converted."[5]

News of this revival spread to Houston, where Mrs. John C. Calhoun heard about this wonderful new experience. "She searched the Word diligently to see if what was reported was scriptural, and decided to visit the scene. Attending the church one Sunday morning, she realized a supernatural power in the songs, prayers, and testimonies . . . and her heart was strangely warmed within her."[6] She soon received the Holy Ghost, with the sign of speaking in tongues.

Upon her return to Houston, she told her pastor, W. F. Carouthers, of the mighty experience she had received. He kindly received it. The congregation was stirred to the depths, and began searching the Word so diligently that two months later, when an evangelistic party came to Houston, this church in Brunner, a Houston suburb, was ready for the new message.

This Houston meeting was a result of Parham's returning to Kansas and Missouri for several short meetings on May 20, 1905. There he enthusiastically talked of the happenings in Texas, and consecrated workers were recruited to go back with him. July 10, 1905 loomed as the day this evangelistic party would leave for the mission field of Texas. Arriving in Houston, this twenty-five-person group quickly set about to have a revival. Bryan Hall was secured, and for five weeks the revival pulsation was felt far and near. The workers enthusiastically preached on the streets and from house to house in the daytime, and then met in the hall for the evening service. The church in Brunner quickly accepted the message and was an extraordinary blessing to the success of the meeting.[7]

Numerous healings were reported, along with the large number receiving the Holy Ghost. One such healing Parham tells us about was that of Mrs. J. M. Dulaney being enabled to walk again. She had been injured in a street car collision two years before, and was confined to a wheelchair. She was carried up the steps into the hall, but thrillingly walked out in her own strength, after being instantly healed. She was known by many in Houston, and it naturally caused quite a large stir.[8]

When the meeting in Bryan Hall was completed it gave time to evangelize neighboring towns with the gospel. Among these were Alvin, Richmond, Angleton, Katy and Crosby. One of the outstanding revivals was held at Alvin, with 134 said to have received the Holy Ghost.[9]

One of the strange and exciting happenings was at the conclusion of a conference in Orchard in April, 1906. Several in attendance had not as yet received the Holy Spirit, and were extremely disappointed because they had not received it at the conference. While enroute to Angleton by train, twelve people, with their hungry hearts crying out to God, were mightily baptized as the train raced along over the prairie. Among that group was Howard A. Goss who would later become a distinguished leader in the Oneness movement. His account reads: "The coach which I boarded was filled with our group, all praying and worshipping God, and soon the Lord really began to pour out His Spirit upon us. That coach became a veritable prayer room!

". . . I knew that several had already been filled when suddenly the power of God struck me! . . . As I lay back limply against my chair, the Spirit of God took possession of my fully-surrendered body, and lastly took hold of my throat and vocal chords in what to me was a new and strange tongue, as the Spirit actually did the speaking. I talked first in one language, which soon changed to another, and then to another. I could tell when the change in the language came, because they were so different . . . About the same time that I had begun to speak, I heard a young lady, Miss Mary Smith, who with her mother was seated facing me, also begin to speak in another tongue. They both had been waiting for the Holy Ghost in Angleton, as well as I. What a time we all had in the Lord. What a train ride!"[10]

During these outpourings several ministers were among those filled, and God was also calling some of the new converts into the ministry. Training was vital, so a Bible school was opened in Houston. A large residence at 503 Rusk Street was rented for this purpose by Parham in December of 1905, and classes began the first of the new year.[11] It was estimated there were some sixty preachers and workers in Texas alone at this time, and though this was to be a short-term school, much good was to come of it.[12]

One of the students was W. J. Seymour, a black Holiness preacher who was very interested in this new message. He was not to receive the Holy Ghost until later, but he held on to every word taught at the school, and must have had an extraordinary memory. In his later teaching it is said he would quote, almost word for word, Parham's classroom teaching. His was to be a prominent place in the propagation of the tongues phenomenon in the future.

But there were others catching the spirit and vision of the hour, and slowly but surely they were going in many different directions, carrying the message that was destined to circle the globe.

[1]Parham, "Parham," p. 95.
[2]Goss, "The Winds of God," p. 12-14.
[3]Brumback, "Suddenly From Heaven," p. 30.
[4]Parham, "Parham," p. 109.
[5]Ibid., p. 108.
[6]Frodsham, "With Signs Following," p. 27.
[7]Parham, "Parham," p. 112.
[8]Ibid., p. 113.
[9]Frodsham, "With Signs Following," p. 28.
[10]Goss, "The Winds of God," p. 43, 44.
[11]Parham, "Parham," p. 135.
[12]Frodsham, "With Signs Following," p. 29.

Chapter 5

The Azusa Street Mission Revival

FROM HOUSTON TO LOS ANGELES

It was 1906, and W. J. Seymour, a black minister, had just received an invitation to conduct a meeting in Los Angeles, California. Not realizing the significance of this appeal, he pondered the strange happenings of the past few weeks. He had been attending the Houston Bible School, conducted by C. F. Parham, and was convinced that although he had thought he was baptized in the Holy Spirit, he actually was not. Being a Holiness preacher, he testified to being saved and sanctified, and considered this the Holy Ghost experience. Now, upon close observation of the Word of God, and a severe scrutiny of the experience of those in the Bible School, he realized that he was not filled as the early church had been. Earnestly he began seeking the Lord to be filled as the disciples of old were.

Now today, this letter of invitation had come. It was from a small black Nazarene church, to whom he had been recommended by a black sister who had recently visited in Houston, and who had been deeply impressed with the humility, preaching and capability of Seymour. Upon arrival in Los Angeles, she had mentioned him to her church, which at the time was seeking an evangelist.

Feeling God in it all, Seymour made necessary arrangements, and caught a train into the unknown west. Sunday morning was to be the first service, and with the turn of events it would also be the last. The preacher chose as his text Acts 2:4, and proceeded to tell the congregation that the scriptural evidence of receiving the baptism of the Holy Spirit was speaking in another language as the Spirit gave the utterance, just as the early church had done on the day of Pentecost.

This ignited a wave of protest, and when Seymour returned for the afternoon service, the door was locked against him. The verdict was that the new doctrine was heresy, and if he was to preach it he would have to preach elsewhere.

As yet he had not received the Holy Ghost either, but he knew that if he preached anything he must preach this truth. Alone in a strange city, with a message no one seemingly wanted, he slowly turned away, but resolved as to the course he must take.

A man standing there, by the name of Lee, couldn't bear to see him turned away homeless, and invited him to his home. It was an uncomfortable feeling for Seymour and the Lees—he penniless, and they, only out of courtesy, with an unwanted guest.[1]

After several days of praying together, the Lees began talking to their guest, and then a Baptist couple, Richard and Ruth Asberry, invited Seymour to conduct prayer meetings in their home at 214 Bonnie

Brae Street.

Things began happening in these prayer meetings, as hearts hungrily sought the blessings of God. Then on April 9, 1906, Lee and six others were rapturously filled with the Holy Ghost, speaking in other tongues. Like a prairie fire it began sweeping out to others, and for three days and nights the service continued, with hundreds of all races pushing into the little house to see what was going on.

Many, as they would step inside, would commence to speak in other tongues, so powerful was God's presence. One testimony by a woman healed of cancer said, "People came from everywhere. By the next morning there was no getting near the house. As the people came, they would fall under the power, and the whole city was stirred. The sick were healed and sinners were saved just as they came in."[2]

Then on April 12, 1906, the man who had started it all was mightily baptized in the Holy Spirit. It has been said that during this three day service the house actually shook under the violent praising of a hungry people.[3]

THE BEGINNING AT AZUSA STREET

After Seymour had received his filling, he realized they must move from the house, as the crowds were so large. A diligent search was made, and there was found at 312 Azusa Street an old building which had formerly been a Methodist church. The two story frame building had recently been a tenement house on the second floor, and on the lower floor was one large room. Located in the vicinity of a tombstone shop, some stables and a lumber yard, no one would complain of all-night meetings.

This was to be the building to house the great three-year revival.

Frank Ewart said, "The writer contacted many of the preachers and workers at Azusa Street in those early days. The news spread far and wide that Los Angeles had been visited by a sweeping revival after the order of that which struck the world on the Day of Pentecost. The conditions that are counted necessary for a real revival were all wanting. No instruments of music were used. None were needed. The choir was substituted by what was called the 'Heavenly Choir.' This singing service was literally inspired by the Holy Ghost. This was perhaps the most supernatural and amazing thing about the meetings.

"Bands of angels have been seen by those under the power of the Spirit at such times of heavenly visitation. Here was one choir without a discord. No collections were taken, but eyewitnesses said that Brother Seymour would go around with five and ten dollar bills sticking out of his pockets, which people had crammed in, unnoticed by him. Food was brought in from day to day for the workers, but no one inquired as to its source. God was recognized as the giver of all, and received all the glory and praise."[4]

One witness, writing of that momentous day, said: "Travelers from afar wend their way to the headquarters at Azusa Street. There they find a two story white washed store building. You would hardly expect heavenly visitations there unless you remember the stable at Bethlehem. But here they find a mighty Pentecostal revival going on from 10:00 o'clock in the morning until 12:00 o'clock at night. Pentecost has come to hundreds of hearts."[5] While services were not in progress many were in prayer, so day and night the deep heart-searching, soul-stirring and genuine devotion was felt at Azusa Street Mission.

One of the astonishing and outstanding things about these meetings was the numbers from so many different churches attending. From everywhere, and from almost all churches in existence, they would come. It had to be what they experienced from God and what they were learning about Him, as there was nothing else to draw them.

"Considering the nature of the services, this success was quite remarkable. Seymour, the recognized leader in the early months, was most unpretentious and humble. He generally sat behind two empty boxes, one on top of the other. He usually kept his head inside the top one during the meeting in prayer. There was no pride there.[6] The speakers, sermons, and subjects were not scheduled in advance, and the meetings followed no formal program. Those in attendance never knew what was coming, since everything was seemingly done more or less spontaneously."[7]

THE SECRET BEHIND IT ALL

There was a secret behind all this, though. There always has to be. God does not come with torrents of blessings unless the price has been paid. In this case, there was to be no missing of the mark.

"A prominent place was given to prayer. The people customarily gathered for an undirected period of prayer before the services commenced. Seymour, upon finishing preaching, would fall upon his knees and begin to pray. Without encouragement, the congregation would follow for long periods of supplication."[8]

Faith for healing ran high, and seekers for healing were usually taken upstairs and prayed for in the prayer room. Many were healed there. There was a large room upstairs that was used. A brother fittingly describes it this way: "Upstairs there is a long room furnished with chairs, and three California redwood planks laid end to end on backless chairs. This is the Pentecostal upper room where souls seek the Pentecostal fulness and go out speaking in tongues."[9]

"For three years the revival continued, going on day and night without a break."[10] No one had dreamed of such an outpouring of the Holy Spirit, especially in such a humble place, but in that period of time people from every continent visited this mighty heaven-sent revival. Nothing like this, with such far-reaching significance, had ever happened in the twentieth century Pentecostal movement, and for this reason the Azusa Street revival is commonly looked upon as the stroke God used to spread the influence of the baptism of the Holy Ghost experience to much of the United States and several countries of the world. "After some time, Seymour was replaced by men of more natural ability, and the races no longer mixed in services, but the flame was spreading far and wide."[11]

"The pioneers at Azusa paid a price for their Pentecostal experience. They fought a fierce battle with the pride that asked, 'Can any good thing come out of such a grotesque situation?' They survived the inevitable doubts that plagued them during moments when fanatical elements threatened to take control. They stood firm against the storm of opposition that swept down upon the little group. It was because of these lionhearted men and women, whose hunger for God and intellectual honesty caused them to accept the Pentecostal message when it was despised by every branch of Christendom, that Pentecost is fulfilling its destiny today."[12]

[1]Ewart, "Phenomenon of Pentecost," p. 37.

[2]Frodsham, "With Signs Following," p. 32.

[3]Brumback, "Suddenly From Heaven," p. 36.

[4]Ewart, "Phenomenon of Pentecost," p. 40.

[5]Frodsham, "With Signs Following," p. 33.

[6]Bartleman, "How Pentecost Came to Los Angeles," p. 58.

[7]Kendrick "The Promise Fulfilled," p. 66.

[8]Frodsham, "With Signs Following," p. 34.

[9]Ewart, "The Phenomenon of Pentecost," p. 42.

[10]Pentecostal Evangel, April 6, 1946, "When the Spirit Fell," p. 7.

[11]Bartleman, "How Pentecost Came to Los Angeles"; Frodsham, "With Signs Following," p. 35-40.

[12]Brumback, "Suddenly From Heaven," p. 47.

Chapter 6

The Spreading Revival

We have noted the beginnings of the outpouring of the Holy Spirit in the twentieth century. We will now take a view of it as it spreads across the country. From far and wide the curious and the hungry had come to Los Angeles, and from there they returned back home to spread the story of their experience and the wonderful way God had blessed at Azusa Street Mission.

The fight was on! The more this message was preached and people embraced it, the more the old line churches fought against it. Leading pastors and evangelists of the day took strong stands against the "tongues movement." Yet nothing could stop it. Ordained of God, heaven-backed, nothing could derail it from its intended purpose of delivering, blessing and aiding the earnest seeker of truth.

OHIO

J. T. Boddy tells what happened in Ohio. "Conventions and camp meetings in the interest of Pentecostal truth were held everywhere, and the fire fell in a remarkable way on these occasions. At one camp meeting in Ohio in 1908, I saw what could not be less than from fifty to seventy people prostrated at one time under the power of God, numbers of whom received the baptism in the Spirit."[1]

NEW YORK

In 1907, a Pentecostal convention was held in Rochester, New York. Miss Susie A. Duncan wrote a glowing report: "Many times the tongues have been understood by missionaries and linguists who have heard the Spirit-filled speak Greek, Hebrew, German, Italian, French, Hindi, Chinese and other languages. A most convincing incident occurred in our midst one Sunday evening. After the opening hymns were ended, John Follette, then one of the students in our Bible school, arose and began to speak with great feeling in the new tongue. After this he burst forth in rapturous song, and then all was quiet. At the close of the service a lady and a gentleman, who were strangers, came to us and asked, 'Who is that young Jew who spoke and sang?' They were surprised to learn that he was not a Jew but a young American. The gentleman then stated that he had lived in Paris and understood several languages. He said that the young man sang and spoke in perfect Hebrew, rendering a Psalm which he had heard in the synagogues in Paris. He said the rendition was impossible to an American; the intonation and variety of expression was unique, and could not be reproduced by a foreigner except in this supernatural manner.

"In the revival in New York at this time," Miss

Duncan said, "we kept a record until the number had reached something like two hundred, then we felt a check in our Spirit as to numbering the people, and from that time desisted.

"Many have received healing as well as the Baptism, and in our conventions testimonies have been given of healing of all manner of diseases."[2]

NORTHWEST

Florence L. Crawford received the Holy Spirit baptism at Azusa Street Mission. In 1907 she departed for Portland, Oregon where she, along with Will Trotter, established a great work. Under her capable and strong leadership several missions in that part of the country were opened, with many coming into the "tongue movement." Soon an "unorganized organization" sprang up, revolving around her Portland headquarters. The Portland group called themselves The Apostolic Faith, the same name Seymour and Parham's groups used, although there was no organizational connection between the three.[3] (Seemingly it was a popular name of the day.)

TEXAS

Howard Goss, a memorable leader in Pentecost says: "Fresh from the revival in Los Angeles, Sister Lucy Farrow returned to attend this camp meeting (held in Brunner). Although black, she was received as a messenger of the Lord to us, even in the Deep South of Texas.

"One day she preached and told about the great outpouring at Azusa Street. After she finished speaking, she prayed for the people to receive the Holy Ghost. The Lord had been using her to lay hands on the people and pray. God would then fill them with the Holy Ghost and speak through them in other tongues. A long line of people queued up before the platform, and as she laid her hands upon each head, one after the other received the baptism of the Holy Ghost and spoke in other tongues. I had not spoken in tongues since my initial experience a few months previous, so I went forward, that she might place her hands upon me. When she did, the Spirit of God again struck me like a bolt of lightning; the power of God surged through my body and I again began speaking in tongues. I have thanked God for this experience all these years, and for the power and privilege of speaking in tongues now at will. I thank God for Sister Lucy Farrow, who later went to Africa as a missionary, and still later, while in Africa, went home to glory."[4]

ARKANSAS

Reports were coming from everywhere of people receiving the Holy Ghost baptism. It was as if the first century was being relived, to see the spreading flame moving so quickly into so many places.

"In 1909 Howard A. Goss and his wife went to Malvern, Arkansas, with a gospel tent, and about three hundred received the marvelous filling of the Holy Spirit in a very short time, several of whom became ministers. The revival continued while many of these went out into other fields of labor with great success in winning souls for Christ. The manifestation of tongues and healings was also present."[5]

It was from this revival that a group of workers went into the community where Samuel C. McClain was teaching school. McClain visited the school to investigate the peculiar things he heard were going on in the revival there. He was so impressed that on the night of his third visit he made his way to the altar, and was excitingly filled with the Holy Ghost.

He said, "On that occasion all this glorious power captured this little unruly member, the tongue, and . . . I began to speak languages I had never heard before. This was the beginning of another great revival in which many were filled with the Holy Ghost. Everywhere people were praying and seeking God for a closer walk in the Spirit—in their homes, fields, groves, barns—everywhere someone was praying through, being baptized with the Holy Spirit. There were also many wonderful healings."[6]

STRANGE HAPPENINGS AT MOODY CHURCH, CHICAGO

Andrew D. Urshan was attending Moody Church in Chicago in this year 1910. At eighteen years of age, in 1902, he had come to this country from Iran to find a new way of life, and now this year he was surely to find it.

A sincere young man, he had been very bold in taking a stand for his Christian principles, preaching to anyone who would listen. Dr. A. C. Dixon, the prominent pastor of Moody Church, gave this intelligent young man permission to use an upstairs room to hold services. He had won some Assyrian converts and, together with them, he would hold services in what they called their upper room. Pentecost fell in this upper room as it had fallen on the early Christians, but naturally with the disfavor of the church. Through this and the subsequent Persian Mission, which was founded after their removal from Moody Church, many of Persian descent were brought into this same experience.[7] A. D. Urshan, although spending most of his long, fruitful ministry in the United States, later sailed back to his homeland as a powerful missionary.

And so it went, pursuing its way. From north to south and east to west the story goes on and on, God having already prepared the way in some places. Many had received the Holy Spirit, not realizing what had come upon them. A. E. Humbard, when a young man, received the Holy Ghost a long time before he had heard of such an experience. Lewis Jones of Albuquerque, New Mexico received his experience and spoke with tongues twenty years before a Pentecostal preacher arrived on the scene.[8] Mightily God moved to spread revival fires.

[1]Frodsham, "With Signs Following," p. 46, 47.
[2]Ibid., p. 48, 49.
[3]Ewart, "Phenomenon of Pentecost," p. 48.

[4]Goss, "Winds of God," p. 56.

[5]McClain, "Students Handbook of Facts in Church History," p. 56.

[6]Ibid., p. 63.

[7]Urshan, "The Witness of God," August, September, October, 1962.

[8]McClain, "Students Handbook of Facts in Church History," p. 58.

Chapter 7

The Finished Work
of Calvary

The pastor of North Avenue Mission in Chicago was wrestling in deep troubled thought. He did not want to give in, but strongly the feeling would rush upon him. Could it be true he had been lacking such a vital ingredient in his Christian life and ministry? Had he been missing the mark and not bringing his converts into the fulness God had intended all along?

MAN OF DESTINY

This was William H. Durham, a man of earnest and intense convictions. He was suffering over the preaching and testimony of those who claimed the baptism of the Holy Spirit, with the initial sign of speaking in a language never learned. What pained him severely was the fact that Scripture backed them so explicitly. After battling for some time, he confessed he must give in to the hunger in his heart for more of God and a heavier anointing on his preaching. He must go to Los Angeles and visit Azusa Street Mission, seeing for himself what this was all about.

The early part of 1907 found him on his way

across the country, this man who was to be benefi-
cially used of God to bring new truth to the hungry
in the plan of God for the last days. Days in which
God would laboriously bring his church to the fulness
of apostolic truth, as was proclaimed and enjoyed in
the first century.

After tarrying for many weeks, he received the
baptism in the Holy Spirit, and his was an overwhelming experience. "He spoke in other languages
with marvelous fluency, and received the gift of interpretation. Pastor Seymour, who had already retired
after a heavy day, was awakened by the Spirit. He
said the Lord had showed him that Durham was to
receive the experience that night, so he redressed and
came downstairs. When he beheld the wondrous sight
of the Chicago pastor filled with the Spirit and speaking in other tongues, the power of prophecy descended
upon him, and raising his hands over Durham, he
prophesied that wherever this man would preach, the
power of God would fall on the people."[1]

THE DIFFERENT PREACHER

Durham went back to Chicago, but this was not
the same preacher. The Holy Ghost baptism makes a
difference, and suddenly his church took on new life.
People came from far and wide and were brought
into this rich spiritual experience. Notables in the
days that were to follow, who received this baptism
in the Spirit at North Avenue Mission, were E. N.
Bell, pastor of a Baptist church in Fort Worth, Texas,
who became the first chairman of the General Council

of the Assemblies of God; and A. H. Argue from Winnipeg, Canada, who was to play a prominent part in the distribution of the message in Canada and the United States.

Something else was noticeable about Durham after his receiving the Holy Ghost in March 1907. He said, "From that day to this, I would never preach another sermon on the second work of grace theory. I had held it for years, and continued to do so for some time, but could not preach on it again. I could preach Christ and . . . holiness, as never before, but not as a second work of grace."[2]

The greater majority in the Pentecostal movement had incorporated the doctrine of two definite and distinct works of grace. At the first work a person received salvation (this was at repentance), and the second work brought sanctification. When people began receiving the baptism of the Holy Spirit, they added a third work. The testimonies would usually begin, "I am saved, sanctified and filled with the Holy Ghost."

THE GREAT DECISION

Durham made a decision to speak out strongly against this doctrine at a 1910 convention. For some time he had studied deeply into this. What he admonished, he called "The Finished Work of Calvary" i. e., sanctification is a continual process received in our initial experience, with a continued setting apart of the believer by the work of the Holy Spirit.

Durham further stated, "I began to write against

the doctrine that it takes two works of grace to save and cleanse a man. I denied, and still deny, that God does not deal with the nature of sin at conversion. I deny that a man who is converted or born again is outwardly washed and cleansed but that his heart is left unclean, with enmity against God in it. This would not be salvation. Salvation is an inward work. It means a change of heart. It means a change of nature. It means that old things pass away and that all things become new. It means that all condemnation and guilt is removed. It means that all the old man, or old nature, which was sinful and depraved, and which was the very thing in us that was condemned, was crucified in Christ."[3]

Quite a lot of confusion was the first reaction to the teaching. Many held out for the second, definite, instantaneous work of grace, and a bitter battle raged, but Durham ploughed on, knowing he had come upon something which would continue to bless the believer.

AZUSA STREET AGAIN

He carried his message back to Los Angeles in 1911 and found once friendly churches closed to him, but undiscouraged he turned to the Old Azusa Street Mission where he found an open door. Suddenly from heaven God used his dynamic personality, his new message and the familiar site of the original outpouring at Azusa to bring believers from all over the area.

Frank Bartleman said, "God had gathered many of the old Azusa workers back to Los Angeles. It was called by many the second shower of the Latter Rain. On Sunday the place was crowded and 500 were turned away. The people would not leave their seats between meetings for fear of losing them. The fire began to fall at Azusa as at the beginning. I attended these meetings with great interest and joy . . . On May 2, I went to Azusa Street, after noon as usual. But to our surprise we found the doors locked, with chain and padlock. Brother Seymour had hastened back from the east and with his trustees decided to lock Brother Durham out. But they locked God and the saints out also. It was Durham's message they objected to."[4]

As has been said,[5] "Seymour had learned from experience that locking the door was an effective way to halt the preaching of an objectionable message in one's mission! He should have learned also that it could not halt the preaching of the message or the fulfillment of his own prophecy concerning Durham."[6]

"In a few days Brother Durham rented a large building at the corner of Seventh and Los Angeles Streets. A thousand people attended the meetings here on Sundays. We had an ordinary congregation of four hundred week nights. Here the 'cloud' rested. God's glory filled the place. Azusa became deserted. The Lord was with Brother Durham in great power. God sets his seal especially on present truth to be established."[7]

The Finished Work of Calvary view spread quickly across the nation and most of the Pentecostal organizations that have formed since, incorporated it in their teaching. The groups in the process of organizing or already organized—the Church of God and the Pentecostal Holiness Church in the Southeastern part of the country and the Apostolic Faith Associations with headquarters in Baxter Springs, Kansas; Los Angeles, California and Portland, Oregon—turned it down. But for the most part and where it really counted, truth had won its battle. Another milestone in the history of the restoration of the church as it was in apostolic days had been passed.

[1]Ewart, "Phenomenon of Pentecost," p. 71.
[2]"The Pentecostal Testimony," June, 1911.
[3]Ibid.
[4]Frank Bartleman, "How Pentecost Came to Los Angeles," p. 145, 146.
[5]Brumback, "Suddenly From Heaven," p. 100.
[6]Ewart, "Phenomenon of Pentecost," p. 41.
[7]Bartleman, "How Pentecost Came to Los Angeles," p. 146.

Howard A. Goss

Howard A. Goss was elected the first General Superintendent of the United Pentecostal Church in 1945 and served until 1951.

Chapter 8

Initial Steps in Organization

That organization would come was inevitable. This movement whose leaders had hoped would sweep into and embrace all faiths found itself on the outside of everything ecclesiastical. With very few churches to preach or worship in, and no authorized group to offer clergy recognition, a movement with so many intelligent and knowing leaders would some way find itself, even amid the biased and prejudiced feelings of many against it, organizing into a systematic, substantial church structure.

WHY ORGANIZATION?

During this early period there were many independent churches, missions and small clusters of people across the country operating on the loosest kind of congregational basis. "Such a polity probably resulted from a concept of spiritual idealism. The constituents believed that the Holy Spirit had been 'poured out' again upon the church, and under His direction the church should function in the way of truth. It became apparent very soon, however, that the Spirit could not lead those persons who would not submit to His administration. Many individuals followed their own inclinations, and, as a consequence, local groups were sometimes in a state of confusion—every person was an authority unto himself."[1] Because of this, many unfortunate things happened to discourage and to destroy what accomplishment had been made.

(1) On the local church level numerous things could happen in situations such as this. Funds were often misappropriated. Congregations were divided by unscrupulous ministers. Trusting Christians repeatedly were the means of having their churches taken advantage of. They needed a process whereby they would know those that labored among them.

(2) As there were no church organizations to back them, missionaries went to the foreign fields voluntarily on their own, but would soon encounter much difficulty. The government of the country would require certain documentation by a recognized organization for owning of property, and for other protections. As S. C. McClain said, "The cry was great for some type of organization in whose name they could build and hold property, and also for some way to prove the worthy and disapprove the unworthy who called themselves missionaries."[2]

(3) The need for joint effort was soon apparent. One lone congregation could only do so much, but several working together could accomplish a tremendous amount more. Missionary endeavor needed the joint effort of many to be the success it should be. Training for young and prospective ministers and gospel workers could be projected through organized

standing together for such undertakings as Bible schools, etc. Vast youth programs could only be effected through co-operative exertion.

(4) The defining of doctrinal position to keep proper equilibrium was felt by some to be essential, and it seemed only proper that some type of central authority would be most helpful in producing the needed results.

All these problems and needs worked in various ways to bring the majority to the realization that even in the face of hostility against organizing, they must move forward to it. As was previously mentioned, a few small groups were already organized at this time, the main ones in the southeastern section of the nation.

Three of these we shall mention here:

THE CHURCH OF GOD

The Church of God of Cleveland, Tennessee had an origin similar to that of other Holiness bodies. The early followers became dissatisfied with their old line church groups, withdrawing to secure closer connection with biblical standards, and then later embracing the Holy Spirit tongues experience.

This body had its founding in 1886, under the leadership of Richard G. Spurling, and was continued after his death by Spurling's son. In 1906, A. J. Tomlinson was elected to the office of Overseer. This group in subsequent years has split into several bodies, but the significant happening was that in 1908, after a year of many of their members receiving the baptism of the Holy Spirit, the annual assembly, which was a small group, accepted the tongues experience into the church. It was at this convention in Cleveland that Tomlinson received the baptism in the Spirit.[3]

THE PENTECOSTAL HOLINESS

The reasoning behind the founding of this church was similar to that of the Church of God, although its present status is due to a merger in 1911 of the Fire-Baptized Holiness Church and the Pentecostal Holiness Church, and then another merger with the Tabernacle Presbyterian Church in 1915.[4]

The Fire-Baptized Holiness Church began its development in the 1880's. Benjamin Hardin Irwin, its founder, said he had received an experience beyond salvation and sanctification, which he called the "baptism of fire" after an experience he had read about in an older Methodist Church. This was accompanied by severe emotional demonstration. The group's later overseer, J. H. King, was in Canada in 1906 and heard of the Azusa meetings through A. H. Argue. He saw that the tenets of the Pentecostals were very similar to his own group, only differing in the evidence of this fire baptism. The Pentecostals believed it was tongues; this body, physical demonstration. That year King, after returning home to North Carolina, and many of his followers received the baptism in the Holy Spirit, speaking in other tongues. This naturally changed their theology concerning the evidence. In 1907 they accepted this tenet in their general convention.

The Pentecostal Holiness Church believing in the

two works of grace—salvation and sanctification, branded the revival in the Fire Baptized Holiness Church, because of its baptism of fire doctrine, the "third blessing heresy." It was founded about 1898, and in 1908 accepted the Pentecostal position of the Holy Ghost baptism. This now united the two groups in doctrine, and in 1911 they were merged in a convention at Falcon, North Carolina. Both bodies were quite small at this time. The other small former Presbyterian group that had accepted the tongues movement joined with them in 1915.

THE CHURCH OF GOD IN CHRIST

C. H. Mason and C. P. Jones, rejected by Negro Baptist groups in Arkansas for what the Baptists considered over-emphasis on holiness, founded the Church of God in Christ in 1897.[5] In 1906, Mason received the news of the Azusa street meeting in Los Angeles. With two colleagues, J. O. Jeter and D. J. Young, he traveled to the west coast and attended the services. Here Mason, during a five-week visit, received the "tongues" experience. Upon returning to Memphis, he found that others of his group had found the same experience. This naturally caused a split in feeling among the church, because some would not go along with this teaching. The leader of the rival faction was C. P. Jones, and in the convention at Jackson, Mississippi, in 1907, when the majority was in sympathy with the Pentecostal faction, Jones and his followers left the church. Shortly in Memphis, at an assembly called by Mason, the Church of God in

Christ was recognized as a Pentecostal body. Through the dynamic leadership of Mason, the church flourished.[6]

WHY NOT ACCEPT THE FINISHED WORK OF CALVARY?

The foregoing can be analyzed as possibly the strong reason why these groups never accepted the "Finished Work of Calvary" revelation. They were already strongly entrenched in the "three works of grace" theory, now having to relinquish their sanctification stand upon receiving light on the baptism in the Holy Spirit. Strong leadership, not willing to take a fresh look at the Scripture, plus a small group, tightly knit together, caused these to stay on the outside of this truth.

OTHER EARLY EFFORTS

(1) **The Beginning Years.** In the early years Parham enjoyed great prestige and popularity among Pentecostals. He was known widely, and preached across the country. Due to this, in 1905 he began holding annual meetings. Although they were very loosely organized, you could call these gatherings some of the first of such type in the movement. Also at this time Parham, under his assumed authority, issued ministerial license. In 1905 Seymour wrote asking for credentials so that he could obtain clergy railroad rates. The name Parham placed on his efforts was "The Apostolic Faith," which many in the begin-

ning called themselves.[7] On the west coast, efforts at Azusa under Seymour, and in Portland under Florence L. Crawford, both assumed this name.

(2) **The Southwest and South.** In the meantime, E. N. Bell, H. A. Goss, D. C. O. Opperman and A. C. Collins were emerging as definite leaders in Texas and surrounding states. Because of their zealous inspiration, annual camp meetings were held in various areas, which brought great harmony to the movement. This spread to other sections of the South, and was one of the main factors in bringing organization.

Needing some kind of recognized authority behind them for credentials,[8] Goss visited C. H. Mason, one of the founders of the Church of God in Christ,[9] a black group, and received authority to issue credentials in the name of that church.

In the meantime, in 1909 a small group organized in Dothan, Alabama. H. G. Rodgers was elected to head the new church, and Wade Ledbetter was the first secretary. This group functioned under the name Church of God, not knowing that there was another church of that same name in Tennessee. In 1912, after it was brought to their attention, they and the large Texas group merged, and retained the name Church of God in Christ. Goss remembered this as more of an association of ministers, because, as he said, "We had no organization beyond a gentleman's agreement, with the understanding for withdrawing of fellowship from the untrustworthy."[10]

As the work grew, it could be seen that more organization was needed to preserve the group standing. "As there was no apparent way to gather up the reins of the different cliques which seemed in danger of galloping off, each in its own direction, Brother Bell and I worked together privately on some kind of solution. We later found that Brother Opperman saw this need too, as did a few others."[11]

THE ASSEMBLIES OF GOD

The crucial moment in the foregoing paragraph was giving birth to the idea of a more substantial and secure organization. Bell and Goss were walking a perilous path, but with the promptings of others, and their own fears for the future of the church, they sat sail upon the given course.

"We realized that great care was needed at this stage, as we had been strictly taught against any form of organization. Irresponsible brethren, if they heard too much, might immediately use the opportunity to poison the saints against us before we could explain, and call us 'compromisers'—a serious charge in those days.

"Of necessity we secretly discussed calling a conference to organize the work. So in November of 1913, Brother Bell and I ventured to announce a conference at Hot Springs, Arkansas, from April 2 to 12, 1914. We signed the original call ourselves." (Goss pastored a church in Hot Springs and, although a young man, he exerted much wise and aggressive leadership.)

"I say 'ventured' advisedly, because we knew that we were likely facing serious opposition, unless God worked mightily. But other leaders took their stand with us, and added their names to the call, which was being published month by month in the Word and Witness. I don't think any of us had many rigid ideas as to how all this should be worked out, but we all supported system against the threatened chaos of the moment."[12]

An immediate storm arose among the 352 people included in this association. Pro and con the feelings ran high but as the time approached for the convention more and more were making plans to attend.[13]

"When the organizational session duly convened, the response proved most gratifying, for between two and three hundred ministers and laymen attended. Of this number, about 120 evangelists and pastors of established churches registered as delegates."[14]

The first conference was blessed by three days and four nights of devotion and fellowship. With the feeling some had, on arrival, against organizing, this was most beneficial. A glorious meeting it was, with a deepening spirit of unity coming upon them. Testimonies of the blessings of God throughout the nation brought much excitement to everyone assembled.

TWO MAJOR PROBLEMS

"Two very difficult matters facing the convention were the establishment of an acceptable system of organization, and the formulation of a doctrinal statement of which the delegates could and would subscribe. What made these formidable problems was the fact that the delegates came from many religious backgrounds, with wide differences in theology and polity.

"The two problems were solved by the general nature of the legislation passed. In matter of organization, a very simple kind of polity was adopted. It was not patterned loosely upon any of the traditional church polities, though it did indicate features of several. The relationship of the local churches to the organization was placed on a purely congregational basis, and through the years the sovereignty of the local church was to be maintained.

"In formulating a doctrinal position, the Constitutional Declaration did not define any specific tenet. The convention felt it sufficient merely to state that the Holy inspired Scriptures were the all-sufficient rule for faith and practice. No matter what their background, all those present could subscribe to such a broad creed."[15]

The only move toward any type of central government was the authorization of an appointment of several men to proceed with any business needed between the meeting of the General Council or annual conventions. Those appointed to the first group were E. N. Bell, J. R. Flower, H. A. Goss, T. K. Leonard, M. M. Pinson, C. B. Fockler, J. W. Welch, and D. C. O. Opperman, with Bell as the General Chairman and Flower the General Secretary. It was decided that Goss would issue credentials to the ministers in the West and South, and Leonard was to do the same in the North and East.

Yes, important things were discussed and decided upon at this convention, but other momentous hap-

penings were taking place in the Pentecostal movement right at this same time, and it would not be
long until weightier decisions would have to be made.

[1]Kendrick, "The Promise Fulfilled," p. 73.
[2]S. C. McClain, "Notes," The Move of God, p. 5, 6.
[3]Mead, "Handbook of Denominations," p. 73, 74; Kendrick, "The Promise Fulfilled," p. 188.
[4]Ibid., p. 171, 177, 182.
[5]"Handbook," p. 76.
[6]Kendrick, "The Promise Fulfilled," p. 198.
[7]Ibid., p. 77.
[8]Brumback, "Suddenly From Heaven," p. 154.
[9]"Handbook," p. 76.
[10]Goss "The Winds of God," p. 163.
[11]Ibid., p. 174.
[12]Ibid., p. 174, 175.
[13]Brumback, "Suddenly From Heaven," p. 154.
[14]Kendrick, "The Promise Fulfilled," p. 84.
[15]Ibid., p. 86, 87.

Chapter 9

The New Issue
(Jesus' Name)

THE WORLD-WIDE LOS ANGELES
CAMP MEETING

Camp meetings have been a strong life line in the Pentecostal movement. Fellowship and inspiration, two ingredients badly needed to keep some people steadfastly progressing, were great helps looked for in attending the summer, spring or fall camp meeting.

The world-wide Los Angeles, California camp meeting in 1913 "fired a shot that sounded around the world."[1] The opportune time had arrived, the anointed preacher was speaking in the pulpit, hundreds of preachers from across the nation and Canada were in the audience. What was this he was saying? What were these conclusions he was coming to? Did he actually mean we had probably been baptizing incorrectly all these years?

This was the popular R. E. McAlister in the pulpit. Unburdening his heart just prior to baptizing several converts, he spoke forcefully on the subject of baptizing as the first-century church had, that is, in the name of Jesus Christ. He emphasized the fact that the words Father, Son and Holy Ghost were never used in first-century baptism.

The message caused quite an emotional upheaval on the platform and in the audience, with one man bounding to the platform, asking the speaker not to preach this doctrine. But the message had gotten across, and although McAlister made an attempt to quiet the consternation of some, this would be the high point of the camp meeting. The preaching of Mary Woodworth Etter, an outstanding evangelist of the era, and the careful count of 364 receiving the Holy Ghost, is now superseded in history by the happenings in the camp centered upon baptism in the name of Jesus Christ.

Frank J. Ewart, who was to play a prominent part of the future propagation of the Oneness message, was in the camp. After hearing Evangelist McAlister on baptism, he invited him to his home to discuss this marvelous truth, making sure of his own message. Ewart was a prominent preacher on the coast at this time, having been associated with William Durham, overseeing Durham's large Los Angeles work prior to Durham's death in 1912, and conducting his funeral.

McAlister's explanations certainly made sense to Ewart, who believed strongly in obeying the Scripture, no matter the consequence, or the price that might have to be paid. Another happening of importance during this meeting involved John G. Scheppe, who became so inspired he spent a night in prayer. Along toward morning he was given a glimpse of the power of the blessed name of Jesus. Leaping to his feet, he ran through the camp, shouting to all the early risers what the Lord had shown him. This experience made a profound impression upon the campers, and all rejoiced with Scheppe, and began to search the Scriptures concerning the "name of Jesus."[2]

AFTER THE CAMP

After the camp was over, Ewart still pondered this new chain of events leading up to his troubled thoughts concerning water baptism and the Godhead, whereupon he and McAlister discussed these questions quite frequently.

Ewart, along with McAlister and Glenn A. Cook as his helpers, opened a revival on Main Street. This naturally threw Ewart and McAlister together often to have their doctrinal discussions. After several months, because suitable buildings were not available, they decided to accept an invitation from Warren Fisher, pastor of a work in Los Angeles, and joined him, assisting in the overall work. A continuous revival progressed, with several of the preachers filling the pulpit mightily through the months. G. T. Haywood of Indianapolis, with his phenomenal knowledge of the Word of God, was especially used of the Lord during this revival.

It was during this time that Ewart noticed the tremendous moving of the Spirit of God when he exalted the name of Jesus. When he would obey God and preach on this great and inexhaustible theme, the power of God would fall and people would flock to the altar.[3] Pastor Fisher and A. G. Garr would urge him to preach on the wonderful name. However, the restrictions were definitely laid down. Ewart said, "We could do many things in the name of Jesus, but were not to do all things in that name." It was at this time that he decided to obey God and step out with His message, which by this; time was clearly defined in his soul.

McClain described it thus, "In the same year, 1914, when the Assemblies of God organization was set up, Frank J. Ewart of Los Angeles, California, through much seeking God in, prayer, had revealed to him through the Word of God a great truth concerning the plan of salvation: that God was in his Son Jesus, reconciling the world unto Himself (II Corinthians 5:19), and that the simple plan of salvation had been plainly laid out by the apostle Peter in Acts 2:38, 'Repent, and be baptized every one of you in the name of Jesus Christ for the remission of sins, and ye shall receive the gift of the Holy Ghost.' It was revealed further that Jesus is the only door of salvation, and that there is none other name given . . . whereby we must be saved (Acts 4:12). Still further it was revealed that all the fulness of the Godhead (Father, Son and Holy Ghost) dwelleth in Him bodily (Colossians 2:9). Thus all the apostles, fully understanding the words of Jesus Christ in Matthew 28:19, baptized every candidate in the 'name of Jesus.' He saw that the apostolic commandment is, 'And whatsoever ye do in word or deed, do all in the name of the Lord Jesus. . . .' (Colossians 3:17)."[4]

EWART'S FIRST ACTS 2:38 SERMON
When Ewart took this decisive action, he met with

Fisher and his assistants, telling of his convictions, and that he did not propose to cause them trouble. The best thing for him to do was to leave quietly, with the idea of pitching a tent on the east side of the city. Fisher acted toward him in a kind way, even helping to furnish the tent, but could not "see" his message, so he bade him goodbye and gave him his blessing.

"The meetings started in the tent on East First Street, just outside Los Angeles, in a town called Belvedere. I preached my first public sermon on Acts 2:38, on April 15, 1914. The message took fire, and that night a revival started."[5]

Cook, an evangelist of note, after making an eastern trip, joined Ewart again, assisting him in this immense undertaking. McAlister had earlier gone into Canada evangelizing. Neither Ewart nor Cook had been baptized in Jesus' name, so they purchased a tank, setting it up in the tent, and proceeded to baptize each other. Crowds began flocking to the tent, interested in being baptized in the name of Jesus.

An unusual characteristic of this outstanding revival was that a large number of those filled with the Holy Ghost were filled immediately after coming up out of the water. They would leave the tank, talking in other tongues.

The sick were brought, and remarkable healings took place. It was as though God had put healing in the water, for many were healed when baptized. It naturally was not the water but the name, and the obedience to baptism by immersion in that name, which brought these mighty manifestations of God's power.

One woman especially fought this revival in a most stubborn way. She passed out tracts before services and endeavored to persuade any she could to not attend the meetings. According to her own testimony in tract form, she was sitting one evening waiting for the service to begin, when a voice spoke to her audibly, "If you will ask my servant to baptize you in My name, I will heal you." She had suffered with inward cancer for some time and was quite swollen. This woman obeyed the voice and came forward, requesting Ewart to baptize her. When she came up out of the water she was completely healed, with the swelling subsiding. They actually had to cover her with a robe and to pin her skirt so as to fit her.

THE TRUTH SPREADS

At this time Ewart was also the editor of a paper, *Meat In Due Season*, which he used to propagate the message of Jesus' name. This paper, which enjoyed a fairly large circulation, went into all parts of the nation and to many mission fields. Through its pages many were convinced of the truth before a preacher ever preached it to them.

After several months with Ewart in Los Angeles, Cook, who had evangelized extensively, carrying the baptism of the Holy Ghost message into many parts of the country, felt led of the Lord to backtrack with the new revelation of God in Christ and water baptism in the exalted name of Jesus. This evangelistic tour into Missouri, Indiana, Oklahoma and some of the southern states brought tremendous results.

G. T. HAYWOOD BAPTIZED

J. Roswell Flower, the General Secretary of the Assemblies of God, heard Cook in St. Louis. After seeing several rebaptized, he became alarmed and wrote to G. T. Haywood in Indianapolis, warning him that Cook was on his way to that city with an erroneous doctrine. Haywood answered, "Your warning came too late. I have already accepted the message and have been baptized." This phraseology was prevalent in that time, and has been handed down even until now concerning this experience and truth. "You came too late; I'm already involved," has been often heard.

Haywood's influence in Indianapolis was extensive, and when he became receptive to this new message, his followers went with him. The count was 465 baptized, with many receiving the Holy Ghost in the water. His church became a center of activity in leadership for Oneness adherents.

The fire that spread slowly over a period of months, now began leaping from church to church and assembly to assembly until it became the issue of the day.

ASSEMBLIES OF GOD OFFICIALDOM'S TRY TO HALT THE PROGRESS

In an endeavor to ward it off and to halt its progress, various means were used. Such an instance occurred "in the spring of 1915, when H. A. Goss called a local conference in Hot Springs, Arkansas to warn young ministers against this teaching on the West Coast. Again E. N. Bell and Goss called a state-wide conference in June 1915 at Little Rock, Arkansas to warn all ministers against this fast-growing move which they believed to be heresy.[6]

Bell, with the written page, fought hard against this so-called heresy. Over and over in the *Word and Witness*, the official Assemblies of God paper, he defended the Trinitarian concept of the Godhead, and Matthew 28:19 as the correct formula for baptism. The doctrinal issue became so hot to handle, that on May 11, 1915 a meeting of the Presbyters of the Assemblies of God was held in St. Louis, to see what would be the best thing to do about this growing trouble that was on their hands.[7]

They, not wanting to establish a creed, issued as mild a statement in the *Word and Witness* against the Oneness and Jesus' name teachings as they could, without overturning their own ship. Bell and Flower both thought, or at least that is what they said in the same paper, that by July it had reached the highwater mark, and would dwindle away. This was only wishful thinking, because before long major events would rock the Pentecostal movement which would send the new issue sweeping to new heights, so that for a short time it would look as if all the Assemblies of God would be engulfed.

E. N. BELL RE-BAPTIZED

During the summer of 1915, the Assemblies of God were beginning their Third Interstate Encampment at Jackson, Tennessee. H. G. Rodgers was the host pastor and Bell was to conduct the camp. Before the camp got underway, Bell said a voice spoke to him saying that if he did not preach water baptism in the name of Jesus Christ in this camp it would be a great failure. Things actually started that way.

The overwhelming evidence for the truth he had been fighting so hard finally prevailed against him, and in a discussion with Rodgers, they decided to send for L. V. Roberts, a noted Oneness evangelist who had been baptized in one of Cook's meetings. Roberts was surprised to receive such an invitation, but remembered that with God all things are possible. He left at once for Jackson and the events that awaited him there.

His first sermon was taken from Acts 2:38, and to his amazement Bell and Rodgers both presented themselves for baptism. This was the start of a mighty deluge of Pentecostal revival in Tennessee and adjoining areas. The influence would be felt at a great distance, for eleven preachers were included among the number of the first to be baptized. On Sunday night Roberts said Rodgers estimated the crowd at 4,000.[8]

Bell's baptism naturally, because of his honored place of leadership, attracted wide attention. The news quickly flew across the nation and into the mission fields. It was met with varied feelings. Some were greatly overjoyed while others were filled with consternation. Still others were so set against the idea that nothing would move them to pursue a new look at Scripture and early church practices. One preacher said, "I don't care if the whole movement swallows this thing; I'm not going to, because it's wrong."

Others had a lot to say, and then were overcome

by their desire to follow the Scripture and leading of the Lord. One such was John Dye, who said, "If I take up this new issue, you can tell the world that I'm crazy." But soon he "took it up," and was still in his right mind. A Oneness paper was received in Camp in August of 1915, telling of Bell's baptism. Evangelist Charles Smith, preaching at the camp meeting in Alto, Texas, of which Harvey Shearer was sponsor, said of W. B. McCafferty, "If Brother Mac goes into it, I'll have to say it's in the Bible." But Smith did not wait for McCafferty. L. C. Hall, who had baptized Smith originally in the titles "Father, Son and Holy Ghost," was soon with Smith in a meeting at Caldwell, Texas, where Hall convinced Smith he should be re-baptized. Smith sent a card to McCafferty, testifying of how the revelation had come to him.

H. A. GOSS BAPTIZED

A General Camp Meeting had been called for August 15, 1915 in Little Rock, Arkansas. A very nice church had been established there, with George Joyner as pastor. L. C. Hall from Zion City, Illinois, who had recently been baptized in Jesus' name, was the camp speaker.

Colossians 2:9-12 was his text throughout the camp. "For in him dwelleth all the fulness of the Godhead bodily . . . complete in him . . . buried with him in baptism."[9]

E. N. Bell was called upon to do the baptizing. Howard A. Goss, on the board of Presbytery of the

Assemblies of God, and a prominent leader in the movement, could no longer stand against truth. Although he had been baptized[10] in Jesus' name by Parham twelve years before this time, he had not realized the significance, but would now accept it fully for himself. He was one of the first baptized by Bell in this camp, along with many lay members.

God has always used various ways of striking truth home to an individual's heart. S. C. McClain, who was in this camp, tells the means God used to finally make him willing to obey the plan of salvation.

"I was in the camp, but like many others saw no need of being re-baptized, although the Lord tried to deal with me in a dream. In the dream L. C. Hall took a large stick of crayon and drew a plain mark straight across the campground. He then lifted his voice, strong and loud, 'Everybody who is going through with God, toe the mark.' I had the financial and business end of the camp meeting, and didn't have the time to consider all the Scripture he was preaching, but that call to toe the mark stuck to me."[11]

Later McClain was preaching a revival in Sheridan, Arkansas. At the close of the meeting several were to be baptized, so to warn them against the prevalent teaching of baptism in Jesus' name, he preached a sermon on the Trinity. A new convert, a woman, had just begun to read the New Testament, and before she had gotten through the first chapter she became very puzzled with verses 18 to 20. McClain said, "Here she was with her finger on these verses with the question. 'Didn't you say last night that God the Father is the first Person, and Jesus is the second Person, and that the Holy Ghost is a third Person?' I answered 'That is right.' Then said she, 'How can the first Person be the Father of the second Person, for Jesus was begotten of the Holy Ghost?' 'Well,' said I, 'that is one of the mysteries of the Godhead; don't worry your brains about that.' But I could not get away from the question." It is needless to say that McClain was baptized in the name of Jesus shortly.[12]

[1]Ewart, "Phenomenon of Pentecost," p. 75-77.
[2]Brumback, "Suddenly From Heaven," p. 191.
[3]Ewart, "Phenomenon of Pentecost," p. 50.
[4]McClain, "Notes," p. 7, 8.
[5]Ewart, "Phenomenon of Pentecost," p. 51.
[6]McClain, "Notes," p. 10
[7]Brumback, "Suddenly From Heaven," p. 194, 196.
[8]McClain, "Notes," p. 10, 11; Brumback, "Suddenly From Heaven," p. 195, 196, 197; Ewart, "Phenomenon of Pentecost," p. 99, 100.
[9]McClain, "Notes," p. 11.
[10]Ibid., p. 3.
[11]Ibid., p. 11, 12.
[12]Ibid., p. 12, 13.

Oliver F. Fauss

Oliver F. Fauss represented the Pentecostal Assemblies of Jesus Christ when they discussed merging with the Pentecostal Church, Incorporated. Later he was elected as Assistant General Superintendent of the Western Zone of the United Pentecostal Church and served in this capacity from 1948 until 1971.

Chapter 10

The Spreading
Oneness Message

There seemed to be no stopping the spread of the Jesus' name Message now. Like the raging flames of a forest fire, it could not be contained. All that its opponents endeavored to do to thwart its fast movement, seemed to add fuel to the spreading flame.

ON TO CANADA

Canada was not left out, so far as the spread of apostolic truth was concerned. First came the outpouring of the Holy Ghost, and then later the revelation of God in Christ and Jesus' name baptism.

In Toronto, in a little mission at 651 Queen Street East, a Mrs. Hebden was baptized in the Holy Spirit in 1906. "She had been praying for more power to heal the sick and cast out demons. The Lord spoke to her concerning the speaking in tongues, but she answered, 'No, Lord, not tongues, but power, power.' She realized that the Spirit of God was grieved and then cried, 'Anything Lord, tongues or anything.' The power of God came upon her and she began to speak in an unknown language."[1]

George A. Chambers, who at the time was a Mennonite preacher in Toronto, said that before long this little mission was overflowing with people. Partitions were removed to accommodate the crowds, and many were filled with the Holy Ghost. New congregations were soon opening in the city, and from there missions sprang up in various places in Ontario and Canada.

It is thought, though, that R. E. McAlister was the first from Canada to receive the Holy Ghost. This was in Los Angeles. He opened a mission in Ottawa later, and was visited with a gracious revival.

A. H. Argue was influential in spreading the message to Canada. After having received the Holy Ghost in Durham's church in Chicago in 1907, he returned to Winnipeg, Manitoba, where he held tarrying services in his home. Soon many were speaking in tongues after being filled with the Holy Spirit. Shortly a mission was opened and the fire began to spread in every direction.

THE FIRST JESUS' NAME MESSAGE
IN CANADA

This set the stage for the "Annual Pentecostal Convention held in Western Canada in Winnipeg in November 1913. This was when the first message on the exclusive rite of water baptism in Jesus' name only was delivered by the guest speaker for that occasion, Pastor R. E. McAlister of Eastern Canada. In those days it was not considered a breach of ministerial courtesy for a guest speaker to advance some new truth. The movement had just undergone a revolutionary process by a new message called 'The Finished Work of Calvary,' and it was therefore at that time in a receptive attitude to receive further revealed truth, should it come. At any rate, the guest speaker very ably analyzed the New Testament Scriptures, proving very emphatically that in every instance the apostles of Jesus baptized once and always in the exclusive rite of Jesus' name."[2]

Frank Small was to do the baptizing that day, and although he had never baptized using that formula before, he proceeded to baptize 30 candidates in the name of Jesus Christ. This was the remote beginning of such baptism in Canada, although neither McAlister nor Small had been baptized in Jesus' name at that time.

L. C. Hall tells of two meetings he and George A. Chambers were associated in. The first began in Toronto on November 14, 1915. "The campaign was opened in a large vacant church building. Our first audience numbered about one dozen, and before the meeting was over it had increased to six hundred. The enemy was busy by pen and voice, warning the people to stay away. 'Heretics' and kindred epithets flew through the air and mails, but the people wanted to know of the Mighty God revealed in Jesus Christ our Savior. Soon the light began to break, and many desired baptism in the 'only name given among men whereby we must be saved.'[3] Eighty-four were baptized, including some preachers. Among them was T. H. Gilbert, a Toronto pastor."[4]

Hall and Chambers went to Berlin, Ontario in

Chamber's own mission, and before this campaign was over, three hundred had been baptized in the powerful name of Jesus.

At this same time G. T. Haywood was preaching for McAlister in Ottawa, and 112 were baptized. History would have us mention this fact: it was Haywood who baptized McAlister, this man who preached the first messages on Jesus' name baptism that began the chain reaction in bringing back apostolic truth to the church in the twentieth century.

TEXAS AND LOUISIANA

A camp meeting was in progress in Merryville, Louisiana. It had begun August 3, 1915. Oliver F. Fauss, a man destined to be a leader in the Oneness Movement, was in this camp as a young man. He said, "It was in the beginning of this camp meeting that our attention was called to an article in the *Word and Witness*, written by E. N. Bell. The name of the article was 'The Sad New Issue,'" He was relating how that some in the upper states had begun baptizing in the name of Jesus only, and he set forth that this was a rehash of an old heresy. Then, during this camp meeting, there fell into our hands the next issue, the August number. In this issue the author of the former article explained that he had been mistaken, in that he had overlooked a truth that God was trying to reveal, and now that God had opened his eyes."[5]

This article, "Who is Jesus Christ," was used of the Lord especially in appealing to preachers to take a fresh look at the Scripture. From this camp and from others (as the Alto, Texas Camp mentioned previously)[6] ministers and workers alike were searching the Bible, making sure of what they believed. Many a heart was searched, and there was much seeking of God for divine guidance.

Harvey Shearer, pastor of a church in Caldwell, Texas, and one of the early day leaders, was in this camp. He and five other workers went from Merryville back across the Sabine River to Caldwell, where L. C. Hall met with them in a tent meeting. Here Hall convinced them of the truth, and they were all baptized in the name of Jesus.

O. F. FAUSS BAPTIZED

In the memory of "old timers" in Louisiana and East Texas, there is a definite high point. It was the Elton Louisiana Bible Conference. This conference lasted through the holiday season of 1915, beginning on the fifteenth of December. The chairman was Shearer, and since he had recently "taken up with the New Issue doctrine" (as they described it in that day), he naturally would have it presented at this conference.

On December 19 the first message on water baptism in Jesus' name was presented. Several who had been pondering this truth became fully convinced, and, at a baptizing later in the afternoon, were buried in "The Name." Fauss said, "As we gathered at the water's edge (a nearby lake), Brother Shearer walked out into the water, and thirteen followed to be baptized, all of them gospel workers or ministers. I was one of the thirteen. Glory to God! We were baptized in the wonderful, glorious name of Jesus, and from that time on there were baptismal services night and day. People were baptized throughout that Bible Conference until it numbered in the dozens."[7]

Robert L. LaFleur, who has been called the "Apostle to Louisiana," was one of the thirteen baptized along with Fauss. His wife, Maude, was one of the six workers baptized in Caldwell, Texas in the L. C. Hall meeting.[8] LaFleur, a few weeks prior to the Elton Conference on the eighteenth of October, had baptized 56 in Jesus' name in DeQuincy, Louisiana, although he himself was not as yet baptized. He at that time, along with Fauss and others, was convinced that Jesus' name was the scripturally founded formula for water baptism.

"On Thursday morning, December 30, Brother H. A. Goss came into the Bible Conference, and his first subject when he spoke was 'Jehovah, the Most Wonderful Name.' He brought out clearly and distinctly how that 'God was in Christ reconciling the world unto Himself.'"

"So great were these Bible studies that they are still remembered by the workers and ministers who attended. The record shows that every minister and gospel worker was baptized in Jesus' name in that conference or soon after, except one. Every church in the northwestern part of Louisiana, and most all in eastern Texas, had baptizings after the conference, where there were from few to scores baptized in the name of Jesus. So great was this truth that seemingly it set the whole country afire."[9]

THE PRINTED PAGE SPREADS
THE GOOD NEWS

"Frank J. Ewart published a paper *Meat in Due Season*, through which many hundreds were convinced of the glorious truth, and were baptized in the name of the Lord. An outstanding Jew was convinced of the Godhead truth and began advocating the true salvation. Abraham Silverstein baptized many in Jesus' name, and printed a paper and books setting forth this truth.

"Daniel C. O. Opperman was editor of a leading paper called *The Blessed Truth*, which did much to carry the truth around the world. Oliver F. Fauss began publishing a very staunch advocate, and later merged it with *The Blessed Truth*. G. T. Haywood, an outstanding black minister who stood high among all Pentecostal ministers and saints, published *The Voice in the Wilderness*. Haywood, a noted Bible teacher, and pastor of one of the largest Pentecostal churches, published several books which were used of the Lord to persuade many. Leading ministers and saints put out other publications and thousands of tracts which convinced sincere people of Bible truths, causing many to be buried in the lovely name of Jesus, and to receive the infilling of the Holy Ghost."[10]

A list of the "big" men who were being rebaptized, and accepting all or part of the Oneness belief about the Godhead, reads like a 'Who's Who' of Early-day Pentecost; E. N. Bell, Howard A. Goss, D. C. O. Opperman, L. C. Hall, G. T. Haywood, H. G. Rodgers, Glenn A. Cook, B. F. Lawrence, Harry Van Loon, and many other outstanding preachers, teachers, and writers. With rare exceptions, most of the Canadian brethren were included in this Oneness sweep. In Louisiana the Assemblies of God had twelve preachers: all twelve departed the Trinitarian faith. Where would this stop? It was becoming a veritable flood, and few had any hopes, or the ability, or the determination to halt it."[11]

Even though the surge toward Oneness and Jesus' name baptism was very pronounced, there were yet huge numbers still held in the grip of tradition, and finding it difficult to break with the teachings of the past. Many were on the very verge, but still lingering, as if hoping someone would pull them back again. While delaying, someone did.

[1]Frodsham, "Signs Following," p. 53.
[2]Small, "Living Waters," April, 1941, p. 1.
[3]Acts 4:12
[4]Small, "Living Waters," April, 1941, p. 6.
[5]Fauss, "Buy the Truth, and Sell It Not," p. 8.
[6]Ibid., p. 56.
[7]Ibid., p. 20.
[8]Ibid., p. 61.
[9]Ibid., p. 24.
[10]McClain, "Notes" p. 14-15.
[11]Brumback, "Suddenly From Heaven," p. 197.

Ministers at 1944 PAJC General Conference

Chapter 11

The Assemblies of God Reject the Oneness Message

During the tremendous surge in 1915 toward the Oneness doctrine, a General Council of the Assemblies of God was held in Turner Hall in St. Louis, beginning on October 1. The proper baptismal formula and the Godhead question were the central topics of discussion. Tuesday, October 5, was given completely to this subject. Two speakers were selected to speak on each side of the question, with Bell and Haywood representing the Acts 2:38 formula, and A. C. Collins and Jacob Miller, the Matthew 28:19 formula.

Each of the speakers went to great lengths to substantiate his own personal feelings in the matter. Each endeavored to convince and make followers of the deeply-concerned delegates to this conference.

After all the preaching, the general feeling of the great majority was to not decide anything at that time. They would wait a year and possibly results coming forth would determine a course of action.

THE DEEP CONFLICT

Those against the message began fighting it very

severely. Great exertions were made to win back those who had gone into Oneness. So the lineup was beginning to take shape: those for and those against. The leaders began exerting great pressure to re-align those who had gone into Oneness, and to keep others behind the Trinitarian teaching. They could very well see the strong possibility of the large majority of the organization going over to the Oneness camp. In harmony with this thinking, one Trinitarian writer, calling the Oneness teaching "Sabellian heresy,"[1] said that "it came within a hair's breadth of capturing the Assemblies of God."[2]

So the fight was on, and everywhere the conflict was raging. This teaching must be stopped. Measures must be drawn up to put an end to the doctrine permeating their midst.

In Houston, Texas young Oliver F. Fauss, just back from the Elton, Louisiana Bible Conference, found a large meeting in progress. His mother, worried about the young man's being recently baptized in Jesus' name, told some of the Assemblies leaders of her son's entry into the "terrible New Issue doctrine," as they called it. Fauss said, "I came into that meeting, thrilled in my heart, life and soul, because I had been buried in the name of Jesus, according to the New Testament plan and pattern as pictured and displayed in the Book of Acts. But when I walked into that building it seemed to me that every 'big shot' of the whole organization leveled his gun at me and shot me so full of holes with so many questions until, as I have made the statement many times, 'I didn't know whether there was one person in the Godhead, or a dozen.'"[3]

This discouraged the young man tremendously. Men in whom he had great confidence were endeavoring rigidly to swing him back again. In his bedroom at home he diligently sought God for guidance, certainly not wanting to be deceived. Being close friends with Raymond T. Richey and his father E. N. Richey,[4] he visited in their home and together they studied this most important question.

Fauss said that after thorough and complete investigation of the Scripture and church history, he could come to no other conclusion but that the Oneness teaching was totally correct, and that the only way baptism was administered in the first-century church was in the name of Jesus.

This is one illustration of many such happenings over the period of months. Pressures were exercised from many quarters. Deep feelings were manifested on both sides of the issue.

THE STRENGTHENING OF ASSEMBLIES OF GOD DOCTRINE

The loose doctrinal structure of the founding ideas of the Assemblies of God organization was being hammered at now. J. W. Welch, who had been chosen General Chairman at the 1915 General Council, declared, along with others, that "some teeth" must be put into a "Pronouncement of Faith." The members of the organization who had embraced the Oneness message were very vocal with it, and, so to speak, "They were driving them, Welch and Company, to the wall." From every corner it seemed they heard of someone else or some church assembly going into this so called "heresy."

Steps were initiated to cause the Oneness message to lose its prestige among the fellowship, and if the advocates of such doctrine would not abandon its propagation, then they would exert all means to cause them to leave the group. Welch, J. R. Flower, T. K. Leonard, D. W. Kerr, along with a few others, were the guiding lights in this definite move to bring the idea to a head.

Every crushing, devastating blow which could be administered was forcibly put forward. It was soon seen that only the strong would stand.

Carlyle said, "Every noble work is at first impossible,"[5] and this was the position the Oneness adherents found themselves in at this point. Old friends and a cherished fellowship were seemingly turning a "frigid shoulder" toward them. This was an impossible end to all their sacrifice and zeal for the Lord's work, but unbearable as it was, the stark reality of it all stared them straight in the face.

It must be said that the Oneness propagators were busy in their tasks also. Under tents and brush arbors; in churches and missions; everywhere a listening ear could be found, they were preaching and telling the story, although it was the desire of those who were members of the Assemblies of God to stay in that fellowship, since doctrine was not a basis on which it had been founded. They remembered very well that the experience of the baptism of the Holy Spirit was the deciding factor at Hot Springs in 1914.

The pressure would now be put upon those who

were the most influential in calling the Hot Springs convention in the first place, namely, Bell, Goss and D. C. O. Opperman. All three had joyfully embraced the "New Issue," and were propagating it everywhere they went.

THE ST. LOUIS MEETING

At last in the June 1916 "Evangel" Welch stated, concerning the coming General Council in the fall, that it would be a decisive meeting, and the Oneness situation would be aired to its fullest extent, with definite lines being drawn. The council was to be held in a small church in St. Louis, Bethel Chapel, from October 1 through, 7, 1916.

Almost everyone in attendance felt "this was it." Something would definitely be decided here. Nervous anxiety was in the air as the first session opened.

T. K. Leonard, S. A. Jamieson, S. H. Frodsham, E. N. Bell and D. W. Kerr were the appointees to a committee which was to draw up a statement of fundamental truths. Bell was chosen to serve on this committee because the leaders detected a wavering on his part as to not taking quite as strong a position on the Oneness doctrine as he had originally.

In committee discussion Kerr seemed to have most of the ready answers, as he had been studying for months how best to refute the Oneness theology. He himself had a few months before almost capitulated to it, but had held tenaciously to the Trinitarian theory, and would now become one of the guiding figures of this convention.

When the committee reported to the council, there

was immediate opposition from the Oneness section. They hopefully wanted to stay with this group, and would do all in their power to remain. They desperately endeavored to strike the strong Trinitarian ideas from these "statements," but they, in turn, were met with the most offensive type of struggle. The die had already been cast, and this naturally was against Goss, Haywood, Opperman and cohorts.

On one occasion "T. K. Leonard facetiously referred to the Oneness doctrine of G. T. Haywood and his colleagues as 'hay, wood and stubble,' with the further remark, "They are all in the wilderness and they have a voice in the wilderness' (referring to the periodical published by Haywood, entitled a *Voice in the Wilderness*). Haywood turned pale and started to rise to his feet for an answer but was pulled back into his chair by those sitting near him. Voices from both sides were raised in protest, and it was minutes before things quieted down and the reading of the report was continued. From that time on, the advocates of the new doctrine took little part in the discussions, having come to the conclusion that opposition would be futile: the tide had definitely turned against them. The prophecy was made, however, that this action of the Council would split the Assemblies of God in two."[6]

THE END OF FELLOWSHIP

The passing of the strong Trinitarian report soon was to mark the end of the close fellowship many had been accustomed to for years. "The Oneness brethren retired to the front of the meeting place, and began to study what they should do. The strong feeling was,

W. T. Witherspoon

W. T. Witherspoon was General Chairman of the Pentecostal Assemblies of Jesus Christ. After the merger Brother Witherspoon was elected as Assistant General Superintendent of the United Pentecostal Church and served until his death in 1947.

"Where shall we go from here?" While they were discussing what steps to take, and which way to turn, the assembly in the hall was singing the old hymn, 'Holy, Holy, Holy, Lord God Almighty, Blessed Trinity.'"[7]

"By the adoption of the statement of basic beliefs, this 1916 council forced the Oneness adherents to propagate their message from outside the Assemblies of God. The list of ordained ministers plummeted from 585 to 429, and the missionary giving shrank proportionately."[8]

One hundred fifty-six ministers and numerous assemblies were expelled that day, to which Oneness men of that hour, still living, say, "It was not because of not believing in healing, holiness, the coming of the Lord, or the baptism of the Holy Spirit with the initial sign of speaking in tongues, but because of the exalting of the name of Jesus according to Scripture."

Bell wavered and stayed with the Assemblies, but Opperman and Goss took their stand. These were the two members of the Executive Presbytery to resign their offices because they could not give up their convictions on Oneness. They were to play a large hand in future years of Oneness history.

[1]Pearlman, "Knowing the Doctrines of the Bible," p. 70.
[2]Brumback, "Suddenly From Heaven," p. 210.
[3]Fauss, "Buy the Truth, and Sell It Not," p. 36.
[4]A prominent Trinitarian in Houston.
[5]"The Dictionary of Thoughts," p. 477.
[6]Brumback, "Suddenly From Heaven," p. 208.
[7]Fauss, "Buy the Truth, and Sell It Not," p. 34.
[8]Brumback, "Suddenly From Heaven," p. 209.

Chapter 12

A Pertinent Question— Could It Be. . . ?

No one connected with the Pentecostal movement in those early days could deny the fact that God was bringing old truth back to fresh reality. All the happenings in the countless meetings across the country were actually not a new thing, but, on the contrary, were as old as the gospel of Christ itself. The early church had experienced them time and again. Through the years, though, prior to the Council of Nicaea in 325 A.D., a turning away from the purity of divine truth and revelation was easily seen. Then in the Dark and Medieval Period of history, New Testament salvation was completely lost, except in the hearts of a few struggling, persecuted people, ostracized as heretics.

Then, like a beautiful ray of sunshine on an otherwise cloudy day, Martin Luther burst upon the scene of history with his Justification by Faith pronouncement. Before his time, bright rays had been seen in the persons of Wycliffe and Huss, and following him came a momentum which could not be impeded, under the guidance of such reformers as Zwingli, Calvin, Knox, Tyndale, Cartwright and Wesley. On into the nineteenth century it seemed something was happening. Slowly and gradually God was bringing old truth back to its proper place. It seemed that one age could only receive a certain amount of truth. It was all they were capable of evaluating, but they would guard it diligently and hand it on to the next era. These, in turn, would take up the torch, and God, seeing fit to add something else more enlightening, would project this on until conditions were such that new truth would be acceptable. Deliberately through the centuries conditions of change from the Roman Catholic concept to a state of mind whereby all the doctrinal activity of the first century church could be comprehended and acted upon was brought about.

PARHAM AT TOPEKA

This brings us to January 1, 1901 in Topeka, Kansas when God began pouring out the Baptism of the Holy Ghost upon the students in Bethel Bible College.[1] This is a pinnacle in history. Much has been said about it and the man C. F. Parham, who was the founder of the school. Here history shows God again revealing himself in tremendous power through the infilling of the believer with the Holy Spirit, with the initial evidence of speaking in tongues as the Spirit gave utterance.

I raise this question, though: Could it be that God was endeavoring to bring a companion truth to light at the same time? Was the Lord of the church attempting to bless countless thousands with divine revelation, but they were unable to grasp the meaning, or were too overjoyed with the Holy Spirit baptism to take time to evaluate the depth of water baptism?

It was the year 1902. Parham wrote a book stating much of his religious philosophy, and the second chapter dealt with water baptism. "Indeed for months nothing, pro or con, came upon the subject, until one day at the Bible School, we were waiting upon God that we might know the scriptural teaching of water baptism. Finally the Spirit of God spoke, 'We are buried by baptism unto His death.' We had known that for years. Again the Spirit said, 'God the Father, and God the Holy Spirit never died.'

"Then how quickly we recognized the fact that we could not be buried by baptism in the name of the Father and in the name of the Holy Ghost, because it stood for nothing, as they never died, and were never resurrected. So if you desire to witness a public confession of a clean conscience toward God and man, faith in the divinity of Jesus Christ, you will be baptized by single immersion, signifying the death, burial and resurrection; being baptized in the name of Jesus, into the name of the Father, Son and Holy Ghost; they are one when in Christ you become one with all."[2]

PARHAM'S ANSWER CONCERNING WATER BAPTISM

Before this time, after trying to put the question of water baptism aside, Parham said, "One day, meditating alone in the woods, the Spirit said, 'Have you obeyed every command you believe to be in the Word?'

"We answered, 'Yes.' The question was repeated;

the same answer was given. The third time the question was asked, we answered 'No,' for like a flood the convincing evidence of the necessity of obedience rushed in upon us, how Peter said, 'Repent and be baptized everyone of you in the name of Jesus Christ.'"[3]

Samuel C. McClain says, "Naturally, as this school and Reverend Parham continued the study of the Book of Acts, it became evident that each and all of the apostles baptized in Jesus' name. In 1902, seeking God very definitely on this subject, Reverend Parham came to the conclusion that a reason why the apostles baptized in Jesus' name was that Jesus is the only door of entrance, that it was Jesus who died, and that Paul declared we are buried with Him by baptism into His death. And, since the Father did not die, nor did the Holy Ghost, it is proper that all candidates be baptized or buried in the name of Jesus Christ.

"In the year 1903 the revival had swept into many cities and villages, and in Galena, Kansas, H. A. Goss was converted and buried in Jesus' name through water baptism'"[4]

In a letter to the author, dated June 15, 1963, H. A. Goss confirmed that Parham did baptize him in the name of Jesus, in the stated revival. Goss was too young and too new in Pentecost to fully understand its consequences at the time.

"After many ministers came into the faith, who used the formula in baptism as had long been used in their former churches, it was decided, in order to keep unity, that the new movement should use the old formula, Matthew 28:19."[5]

Now, as one looks back upon such history, the

pertinent question arises time and again: could it be that this was God's time to bring this glorious truth to the surface, whereby all professing Pentecostals would be practicing it today? Were men too enveloped in feelings of unity to stand for heaven-sent revelation? Could it be that much heartache and agony gone through later would have been avoided, if proper action had been taken, and pointed direction had been given at such a time as this?

[1]Ewart, "Phenomenon of Pentecost," p. 30.
[2]Parham, "A Voice Crying in the Wilderness," p. 23, 24.
[3]Ibid.
[4]McClain, "Notes," p. 3.
[5]Ibid.

Chapter 13

Beginnings In Oneness Organizational Efforts

The Assemblies of God rejection left a large number of Oneness ministers without a church to unify their efforts. The issuing of credentials and a unified missionary effort had to be considered, so steps were immediately initiated to organize.

It must not be assumed, though, that all the Oneness ministers were in the Assemblies of God, as many had never joined this church group. Such men as Frank J. Ewart and Harry Van Loon had not, but were in close fellowship with the others.

THE GENERAL ASSEMBLY
OF THE APOSTOLIC ASSEMBLIES

"During the Christmas Holidays of 1916, saints and ministers were arriving in Eureka Springs, Arkansas by great numbers. Reverend Daniel C. O. Opperman and Mother Barnes had already opened a Faith Bible School in a sixty-one room hotel building on Spring Street."[1]

The need for an organization was so urgent that one was formulated at this time, which began issuing credentials immediately. Samuel C. McClain's credentials were dated January 26, 1916. The name decided upon was the General Assembly of the Apostolic Assemblies. Opperman became the General Chairman and Goss was made the Secretary.

The war clouds of World War I were hanging low, and steps were initiated to provide proper recognition for the ministers of military age. To their astonishment, they found they had organized too late for this recognition. This was to be the impetus for the next move in Oneness organizational historical structure.

THE PENTECOSTAL ASSEMBLIES
OF THE WORLD

On the west coast a minister by the name of Frazier organized a group of Oneness people under the name of Pentecostal Assemblies of the World, in late 1914. This was a small group, and confined mostly to the coast, with headquarters in Portland, Oregon.[2]

The significant happening at this time in this group was the acquiring of the proper recognition by the government for its military-age ministers. This was what the new organization, The General Assembly of the Apostolic Assemblies lacked, and casting about, they found this small group and their highly-valued prize. Immediately negotiations were initiated for some kind of workable agreement.

These negotiations were diligently pursued, and a merger of the two groups was adopted in late 1917. C. W. Doak was chosen to be the General Chairman, with G. T. Haywood becoming the Secretary-Treasurer.

The new organization chose to continue the name of the Frazier group, The Pentecostal Assemblies of the World.

A UNIQUE FELLOWSHIP

This was to prove a unique fellowship for several years, because both white and black were members. Doak was a white man and Haywood was black. Haywood had been an influential man for years first among the Trinitarians, and after seeing the light on the Oneness message, he was greatly respected among Oneness people.

He pastored one of the largest Pentecostal churches in the world, in Indianapolis, Indiana. Through his ministry, hundreds, both white and black, had been won to the Oneness truth and baptized in Jesus' name. His influence as one of the top leaders in the church helped to unite the races in this great effort.

McClain speaks of this fellowship thus, "Throughout the north and east there seemed to be very little, if any, race prejudice. I, being southern born, thought it a miracle that I could sit in a service by a black saint of God and worship, or eat at a great camp table, and forget I was eating beside a black saint, but in spirit and truth God was worshipped in love and harmony."[3]

For several years this worked very well, with a considerable growth and a wonderful unity, but in later years dissatisfaction began to rise between the two races, seemingly over misunderstanding by the younger northern black ministers of the question of segregation in the South.

"While all Spirit-filled ministers agreed that with God there is not a color line and in the hearts of the people of God there should be none, yet ministers laboring in the South had to conform to laws and customs."[4]

All the conventions of the Pentecostal Assemblies of the World were held in the North, due to segregation in the South, and it was only natural, due to long distances of travel in that era especially, that not nearly as many Southerners were in attendance as Northerners. When legislation to be considered would arise that was very vital to the church as a whole, the southerners were usually outnumbered. A goodly number of the northern ministers were black, so, unfortunately, a spirit of agitation began to arise, pitting, to a degree, the races against one another. The Southerners wanted a convention closer to their area, but this could not be done because of the racial feeling in the South toward integration. All these things began working against the structure of the Pentecostal Assemblies of the World.

The Assemblies of God were not having this trouble because they, at this time, were made up primarily of white people. The Trinitarian Church of God in Christ also avoided this, because they were primarily black. This would, in time, be the pattern among the Oneness movement also.

There was also another problem during the above crisis, that caused considerable agitation. On a larger scale, the Oneness people have always held high standards of holiness, and the latter part of the name of their church disturbed them. The apostle John had said, "Love not the world, neither the things that are in the world,"[5] and constantly preachers of the gospel were hammering away at the love for worldly accumulation. The "Of the World" part of the name caused great dissatisfaction, with many claiming "that a church organization should not be called 'Of the World.'"[6]

THE SOUTHERN BIBLE CONFERENCE

S. C. McClain was pastoring in Fort Smith, Arkansas, and W. A. Mulford was conducting him a revival. "They felt the need of a great spiritual gathering, where all could worship and draw near to God in spiritual fellowship. These two sent out a call for such a gathering, and called it the 'Southern Bible Conference.' This conference was held in Little Rock, Arkansas in 1921, in an old Presbyterian Church near the State Capitol, on the corner of Fifth and Victory Streets."[7] Until recently, there was a thriving Oneness Church at this location, which the late G. H. Brown pastored for many years. R. G. Cook, who was to become one of the Assistant General Superintendents of the United Pentecostal Church, was pastor at the time in the city.

"Daniel C. O. Opperman, who had served as President of the Ozark Bible and Literary School, was chosen Chairman and Moderator of the Bible Conference. The response was great, with ministers and saints from many states coming, and the spiritual uplift was beyond expectation. There were no business sessions, as they had met for spiritual food, and God had not failed them, as a rich spiritual table was spread. The fellowship and worship was so wonderful that some sent telegrams to other ministers, who soon joined the people that know the joyful sound (Psalm 89:15). Mulford wired E. W. Doak, then presiding Chairman Bishop of the Pentecostal Assemblies of the World, who took the next train to Little Rock.

"The fellowship and spiritual uplift was so great, along with deep consecration, that William E. Booth-Clibborn printed a booklet called `Dust and Ashes,' giving a fine account of this glorious gathering. Many healings were manifest. Seekers for the Holy Ghost baptism prayed through. There were no certain speakers, yet God used Booth-Clibborn in a mighty way, and Opperman presided under the leadership of the Spirit."[8]

This convention was to be remembered a long time, and its tremendous blessing would play a prominent part in the future of the Oneness movement. The strength derived from its unity had not been enjoyed in any recent conference, and this was to have its far-reaching repercussions.

THE ST. LOUIS CONFERENCE, 1922

"Because of the sweet spirit of uplifting fellowship in the Southern Bible Conference, it was suggested, and E. W. Doak agreed, that the first part of the next conference of the Pentecostal Assemblies of the World be given entirely to worship and consecration. This was to be a time of digging deep and seeking God for more love and unity. But someone made the mistake of designating those days as a continuation of the Southern Bible Conference.

This did not work, for naturally the black brethren had had nothing to do with that part of the services, and the conference was nothing like in spirit as it was hoped to be."[9]

This is readily understandable, because tension would naturally be created in such an atmosphere as existed there. The wedge was being driven deeper, and soon it would break the organization into several parts.

It was at this convention that many of the white leaders decided that peace and fellowship would be God's will for them, and gradually thoughts began settling upon leaving the Pentecostal Assemblies of the World for the black, and founding a new organization. The general feeling was that under the present setup a spirit of discouragement was received, instead of the inspiration so needed in propagating the gospel of salvation.

In 1924 in St. Louis, at the General Conference, it was decided the time had come. Hungry to have love and unity prevailing, and to be a looked-for ingredient in their conventions, a group of the leading white ministers met in the basement of the conference building to discuss plans for the future.

"Thus came plans in a basement gathering of white ministers to let the black brethren, under the able leadership of Elder Haywood, carry on with the Pentecostal Assemblies of the World, while all the white ministers would organize another association to meet the needs of the South."[10]

[7]McClain, "Notes," p. 17, 18

[2]Ibid., p. 18.
[3]MCClain, "Notes," p. 18, 19.
[4]McClain, "Notes," p. 21.
[5]I John 2:15
[6]McClain, "Notes," p. 21.
[7]Ibid., p. 22.
[8]Ibid., p. 22, 23.
[9]Ibid., p. 24.
[10]McClain, "Notes," p. 24, 25.

Chapter 14

Other Oneness Organizations

In this chapter we shall devote our thoughts to those formative years from the events of the last chapter to the formation of the United Pentecostal Church. Many happenings are in evidence to bring about such a merger of strength over those twenty years of time. It must be remembered that this is an area of Oneness history that nothing whatsoever has been written about. As a historian, I have pursued various sources to dig up the events that are recorded here, and I must admit it has not been an easy task. Several who could have gone into more detail have already passed on to their reward, but others have willingly helped, and I am most grateful.

THE PENTECOSTAL MINISTERIAL ALLIANCE

A. D. Gurley wrote, "The Pentecostal Ministerial Alliance began its formation in October, 1924 in the city of Chicago, at the invitation of Pastor A. D. Urshan. It was actually considered at this time to begin an organization called the Apostolic Church of Jesus Christ.

"From this meeting, Whittington began the Apostolic

Church of Jesus Christ in St. Louis, and the Pentecostal Ministerial Alliance was founded in Jackson, Tennessee. However, it was 1925, when it was actually organized and named. There were two General Conferences in 1925, the first one was held in Jackson, Tennessee in the month of February. The second one was in St. Louis, Missouri in October."[1]

McClain states that, "It was not intended to be a general church organization but an alliance of ministers, merely to care for all the needs of the ministry, and that every local church with its pastor was to be a sovereign government of its own."[2]

To head this new alliance of ministers, the prominent evangelist L. C. Hall was chosen as General Chairman. To fill the Secretary-Treasurer office, Howard A. Goss was selected. Later he was to be asked to step up to the chairmanship.

This loosely-organized alliance of ministers was to continue for several years, with continual growth and blessing, until a stronger incorporation was formed in 1932.

THE EMANUEL'S CHURCH IN JESUS CHRIST

There was quite a lot of dissatisfaction, though, with the Pentecostal Ministerial Alliance in some quarters. It was thought by many to be too loosely organized, and also too open for people who did not believe in the Oneness message and the truth of baptism in the name of Jesus.

Many, wanting to take a much stronger stand on this giant issue of the day, decided to bring together another church group that would strongly adhere to this idea.

In a Tri-State Conference, representing Oklahoma, Louisiana and Texas, held at Houston, Texas in October of 1925, plans were laid to do so. From this beginning the Emanuel's Church in Jesus Christ came into being. The Chairman was W. H. Lyon, and the Secretary was G. C. Stroud. O. F. Fauss was a third member of the board of organization. A. D. Urshan was in this convention, and encouraged its conception. Urshan was a very popular speaker of that era and had a great amount of influence.

A SIGNIFICANT HAPPENING

An event that changed the course of many churches in Louisiana and Texas for almost twenty years took place in 1927, when a difference of opinion arose among the brethren of the Emanuel's Church in Jesus Christ. Several of the ministers and churches in Louisiana and Texas decided to leave the Emanuel's Church in Jesus Christ and take membership with the Pentecostal Ministerial Alliance. Certainly the PMA was happy to have this sudden windfall. Their representation in these two states became, overnight, quite large. This tells the story of the two divergent groups in these areas through the next two decades.

Gradually across the nation the two groups were planting churches. Sometimes in the same cities there would be churches representing both organizations; this becoming more prominent later, when the two were known as the Pentecostal Church, Incorporated and the Pentecostal Assemblies of Jesus Christ.

APOSTOLIC CHURCHES OF JESUS CHRIST

About the same time the Pentecostal Ministerial Alliance and the Emanuel's Church in Jesus Christ was being thought about, another endeavor in organization was being considered. After the Chicago meeting, W. H. Whittington and Ben Pemberton became convinced of the need, and "incorporated a small work in the city of St. Louis in 1925, and chartered it under the name of Apostolic Churches of Jesus Christ."[3]

THE BEGINNING OF CONSOLIDATION

Sincere, honest and Spirit-led men are peaceful men. They endeavor to keep peace in the overall polity, even when minor differences arise. If they can find a peaceful solution, they will pursue that end. This is not to say that principles will be forsaken and convictions will be rudely thrown aside, but to the contrary.

Basically, most Oneness people have believed in repentance, baptism in the name of Jesus and the receiving of the Holy Spirit with the initial evidence of speaking in tongues, along with a consistent life of holiness. These have been the cardinal truths which have rallied these people together from the beginning. From this time on, we shall gradually see a coming together of the people of this distinct biblical truth.

In 1927, the Emanuel's Church in Jesus Christ and the Apostolic Churches of Jesus Christ met in Guthrie, Oklahoma, to see if there were possibilities for a merger of the two groups. Things worked out very well, and the next year, in October of 1928, in Port Arthur, Texas, at a General Convention, the Emanuel's Church in Jesus Christ and the Apostolic Churches of Jesus Christ came to the conclusion that it would be best if they were to walk together from that conference on. These churches continued to use the name Apostolic Churches of Jesus Christ until 1932, when another merger was enacted.

Chosen as Chairman was O. F. Fauss, and the Secretary's position was filled by W. H. Whittington. E. D. Browning was chosen as Treasurer.

THE SECOND MERGER
OF ONENESS CHURCHES

In the years of 1924, 1925, and 1926, when the machinery was being set up for the formation of the new organizations, the Pentecostal Ministerial Alliance, the Emanuel's Church in Jesus Christ and the Apostolic Churches of Jesus Christ, not all the white ministers of the North went along with any of these groups, preferring to stay with the Pentecostal Assemblies of the World.

Friendships, knit by the like experience of the New Birth and previous fellowship, still existed strongly between the various members of all the organizations, and many preached revivals and special meetings in the other groups. All this would naturally, lead, from time to time, to contemplations about getting back together.

THE PENTECOSTAL ASSEMBLIES
OF JESUS CHRIST

It was decided that the Apostolic Churches of Jesus Christ and the Pentecostal Assemblies of the World would meet to work out a merger of their groups and, consequently, their efforts in the work of the Lord. In November of 1931 in the city of St. Louis, a conference was convened for this purpose. The merger was adopted, and they took a part of each of their names to appropriately name the new organization. This new name was The Pentecostal Assemblies of Jesus Christ, commonly known as the PAJC. The leadership was composed of a Board of Presbyters who, in turn, would elect one from their body to preside at each General Conference. J. A. Frush was the Editor; a black man, Karl Smith, was Secretary.

This merger did not work as planned, because almost from the start, hindrances arose to hamper the proposed idea. The organization forged ahead, gaining strength and ground, but the same type of difficulties encountered in the old Pentecostal Assemblies of the World were again run into.

Bishop Grimes, a prominent black leader, did not accept the idea of the merger, so he left the conference and renewed the Pentecostal Assemblies of the World charter before its expiration. This caused quite a bit of unrest, and several decided to go along with him.

Then it was perceived that the same distasteful experience as before, concerning the races, was to be gone through. Due to segregation in the South, a General Conference could not be held below the Mason-Dixon line with all in attendance, and the re-enactment was on.

It was decided, though, that a conference would be held in Tulsa, Oklahoma in 1937. This proved to be the undoing of relationships with the arrangement worked out in 1931 at St. Louis. Only the white ministers were able to attend, and only legislation of a minor order was to be passed upon, and that to be sanctioned the next year in a conference held again in the North, with all members present.

This could not work out harmoniously. Some felt that they were being discriminated against, even though this was not the spirit of the happenings at all. Nevertheless, the PAJC lost several, with most of the black brethren going back to the old Pentecostal Assemblies of the World.

The next convention in 1938 was held in Columbus, Ohio, with O. F. Fauss presiding. It was decided that the organization would return to the governmental General Chairman again. W. T. Witherspoon was selected to be the General Chairman and the Secretary-Treasurer's position was filled by Stanley R. Hanby. This proved to be very strengthening and workable, and the PAJC "moved ahead in a progressive manner,"[4] until its merger with the PCI, to form the new vitalized United Pentecostal Church.

THE PENTECOSTAL CHURCH
INCORPORATED

The Pentecostal Ministerial Alliance, which, since 1925, was a loosely organized association of ministers, felt in 1932 that a change would help them propagate the gospel. It was generally felt that a stronger organizational setup would further their ends to a greater degree for future growth.

In Little Rock, Arkansas, at the General Convention, legislation was enacted to organize more fully, and also to "include the local churches as an integral part of the organization."[5] The name was changed to Pentecostal Church, Incorporated and was commonly called the PCI. B. H. Hite was selected to fill the position of General Chairman in the new organization. W. E. Kidson, who was serving as the Secretary-Treasurer of the PMA, was also re-elected to that office.

The Pentecostal Church Incorporated was certainly progressive minded, and moved along strongly. Although perhaps not conscious of the fact, it was (as was the PAJC) moving forward, with every step, toward the most progressive leap of all, when it would unite together with the PAJC, and become the United Pentecostal Church.

[1]Gurley, "Letter to Author," May 21, 1963.
[2]McClain, "Notes."
[3]Gurley, "Letter to Author," May 21, 1963.
[4]Gurley, "Letter to Author," May 21, 1963.
[5]Ibid.

B. H. Hite

B. H. Hite served as General Chairman of the Pentecostal Church Incorporated and along with others was influential in the merger of that church with the Pentecostal Assemblies of Jesus Christ, Brother Hite died in 1948 not long after the merger.

Chapter 15

The United Pentecostal Church

The various events of the years following the Oneness twentieth-century advent into organizational effort would naturally develop into resolute feelings for a united endeavor to proclaim the biblical message.

The mutually strong love for the biblical truths of the fullness of the Godhead in Christ and baptism in the name of Jesus were a constant source of drawing these people together. Oneness adherents readily admit that many who have come into the movement have not appreciated the value of the message as fully as others, but emphasize that most converts have ardently loved the truth. It was this holding to beliefs not generally accepted or fully valued by the multitudes that caused a oneness of feeling and affections of kinship toward people of like precious faith.

It was in the year 1939; the place, Houston, Texas. An automobile driven by O. F. Fauss was headed in the direction of the depot, and in the back seat sat two men, deeply engrossed in conversation. Fauss remembers the meeting well and, speaking of it, said, "W. T. Witherspoon, General Chairman of the PAJC, was preaching for me here in Houston, and I thought it would be a good idea, since the PCI headquarters were located here, to get Brother Witherspoon and the General Superintendent of the PCI, H. A. Goss, together for a visit. So, while taking Brother Witherspoon to the train depot, I stopped by the PCI office and invited Brother Goss to accompany me to see Brother Witherspoon off."[1]

Fauss remembered, with a twinkle in his eye, that this short visit between these two influential leaders helped cement strengthening ties between them, and thus to bring their two divergent churches closer together.

THE ST. LOUIS CONFERENCE

In late September, 1944, the General Conference of the PAJC was convening in Pastor Walter S. Guinn's White Way Tabernacle in St. Louis, Missouri. Harry Branding, an honored leader of the PCI, who also pastored another thriving church in the city, visited in this convention. Knowing Fauss had quite a lot of influence, he approached him with the idea of a merger. His words were, "Why not get together?" He told Fauss that if the PAJC would pass some kind of legislation toward it, he would use all the power he had to accomplish the same end in the next conference of the PCI.

This made Fauss extremely happy, and he, along with others, set the machinery to rolling. The resolution committee reported to the convention on September 30, and under the able guidance of General

Chairman W. T. Witherspoon, the conference, after strong questioning, many doubts and close observation, passed a resolution extending an invitation to the PCI for a meeting with the officials of the PAJC.

Action on this resolution caused a sudden wave of speculation and questioning, but for the most part it was enthusiastically received, and the PAJC began looking forward to the PCI conference, less than a month from that time.

THE JONESBORO, ARKANSAS CONFERENCE

News travels fast, but not all the delegates to the Jonesboro conference knew of the PAJC invitation. Talk of such a union had smoldered for years, but definite action to consider was a surprising factor at this convention being held in Bible Hour Tabernacle (pastored by T. Richard Reed), and presided over by the General Superintendent, H. A. Goss.

As ministers and delegates from various parts of the country began arriving, the invitation immediately became the foremost point of conversation. Everything became secondary in the face of such a possibility.

When finally the resolution was presented for acceptance of the invitation from the officials of the two church groups to meet for an exploratory session, it had already been pretty thoroughly discussed, pro and con. Now on the floor it received close scrutiny also. As was the prior feeling in the PAJC conference, it was the generally accepted sentiment that nothing could be lost by a meeting such as this, and always the great possibility loomed that this could be one of the best things that could happen.

"On October 27, a resolution was duly adopted to accept the invitation from the PAJC, and authorizing a committee of officials to meet with the officials of the PAJC to discuss the terms of agreement."[2]

HINDRANCES TO SUCH A MERGER

There were many strong ties between these two churches which would have a natural tendency to draw them together. These were discussed often, and always led individuals in both churches to sentimentally long for some type of co-operative effort.

On the other hand, there were other feelings between them that had succeeded in dividing them, when most of the older ones came out of the P.A.W. in 1924, and had kept them apart up until this time.

THE NEW BIRTH QUESTION

Back in the late teens and mid twenties, there arose two different beliefs concerning the essentiality of water baptism in the name of Jesus. Some believed it to be an essential element in the new birth, while others, believing it to be Bible truth, did not believe it to be essential to a new birth experience.

Either side of the question would bring them to a belief of who would make up the bride of Christ? Those who took the stand for the essentiality of water baptism naturally were persuaded that only those who had obeyed the complete Acts 2:38 plan could be ready as the bride to go in the rapture of the church. Those who did not take this position felt that the baptism of the Holy Ghost was the essential ingredient needed, and that all people, whether Oneness or not, who had received this experience, would make the rapture.

The above paragraph presents the general idea in the divergent opinion concerning Bible salvation. Other doctrinal points contributed to a difference of feeling also. The "light" message was held by many, and in this it was believed that God required of you, concerning the new birth, only according to the amount of light which had been revealed to you. Repentance was all right if the light on water baptism in Jesus' name and Spirit baptism with the initial sign of speaking in tongues had not as yet been seen. The requirement was that as light was revealed, it must be accepted and walked in.

Holiness standards concerning modest attire and worldly pleasures were other points of differences in some localities too, but the major point of distinction at this time was over the new birth question. The word "compromiser" was very loosely thrown around in those days, and was used against almost anyone who did not see things quite so strongly as the other person involved.

As a whole, the PAJC took a firmer stand on the new birth; and while the PCI did not take as strong a stand, there was a large segment in their church that believed similarly as the PAJC majority.

WHAT WAS THE ANSWER

These were the dividing lines, and how to work them out was the big question. But it turned out that this was not to be as difficult as first believed. After pursuing several involved areas, general agreement began materializing.

Inge said, "The wise man is he who knows the relative value of things."[3] So it was that this capacity to see the value of harmoniously striving for the same end, would develop into one of the leading factors of merger.

All believed that the Acts 2:38 message must be propagated to the ends of the earth. All believed this could best be done with the joint effort of the two churches. All believed, because God was with them, that they could work together so the world could be touched with the Oneness message. With these noble ideals in mind, they began their approach to the other problems.

AN IMPORTANT DISCOVERY

What about this new birth problem? What about the holiness ideas? These serious issues must be faced, and wisely they must be considered. As each organization began its close scrutiny of the other, it was discovered by the majority what others had known and seen for some time: that there were people and beliefs in their own group on a comparative line with those in the other group. If they could fellowship those in their own organization, why couldn't they show the same brotherly respect to those in the other? If they would accept them in the fellowship they were already a part of, why couldn't they somehow find a way to do the same to godly men from the other church?

These were questions they pondered, long and hard, recognizing that so much depended on their ability, as men of God, to answer these questions properly. The future depended upon the decision that eventually would come from this thinking. Young preachers, some just beginning their ministries, while others were yet "growing on the vine," would be affected all their lives by the resultant agreement or disunity. These were essentially the considerations pondered deeply by all concerned.

THE SUMMIT MEETING

The spring of 1945 was to be a time of vast importance. The meeting of the officials of both organizations was to be convened, and the momentous discussion of merger would envelop them. The future of many thousands of people hinged upon what would come out of these discussions. Thousands of souls yet to be won in subsequent years would be affected by the events breaking forth from this vital summit meeting of Pentecostal ecclesiastical leaders.

Representing the PAJC were W. T. Witherspoon, General Chairman; Stanley R. Hanby, General Secretary-Treasurer; and O. F. Fauss. Representing the PCI were Howard A. Goss, General Superintendent; Oscar Vouga, General Secretary-Treasurer, and B. H. Hite.

Witherspoon, Goss and Fauss have already had an introduction to this history, but Hanby, Vouga and Hite are newly thrust upon the scene. They were not strangers on the Pentecostal scene, however, as each had labored diligently in the past, and from that faithful service had been called upon to shoulder the heavy responsibility they carried into this meeting. Later in the merged

United Pentecostal Church, Vouga would become an Assistant General Superintendent and then the Director of Foreign Missions. Hanby would later become the first Director of Home Missions. Hite did not live long after the union of the two churches, but was to have an honored place in formulating the merger. He was a former General Superintendent of the PCI.

The meeting was held in the city of St. Louis at the Milner Hotel in 1945. Some apprehension was felt on both sides, as feelings had been expressed that nothing could be acceptably worked out between them, so a tenseness was in the atmosphere. After some time of deliberation, with seemingly not too much accomplished, Hanby stood and asked a simple question which seemed to clear the air and pave the way to thinking along the same lines expressed in both churches' General Conferences.

His question was, "Do you really want to unite? Is there actually a desire for a merger of our two churches?" Stunned, the brethren plunged deeply into the question, for inspiration of the past which had given each of them aspirations for such a move, had brought them to this place of contemplation.

THE FUNDAMENTAL DOCTRINE

Hearts began to warm, and the lofty ideals of past discussions began throbbing again. Seemingly a fierce determination gripped each of them to see this through. The old adage, "Where there is a will there is a way," became uppermost.

Finally Witherspoon retired to a private room for awhile with pen and paper, coming out shortly with the Fundamental Doctrine Statement, which all immediately seized upon as from the Lord. It read, "The basic and fundamental doctrine of this organization shall be the Bible standard of full salvation, which is repentance, baptism in water by immersion in the name of the Lord Jesus Christ, and the baptism of the Holy Ghost with the initial sign of speaking with other tongues as the Spirit gives utterance.

"We shall endeavor to keep the unity of the Spirit until we all come into the unity of the faith, at the same time admonishing all brethren that they shall not contend for their different views to the disunity of the body."[4]

It was fully agreed that this should be acceptable to all as a declaration for Oneness people everywhere. A feeling of victory permeated the room now, and carried on into other discussions upon serious angles to be worked out suitably.

THE NEW NAME

The question of a name was to take some time, because everyone recognized that "A good name is rather to be chosen than great riches."[5] Several names were presented, with each receiving its due regard. Someone presented the question: would it be better to get away from the word Pentecostal? This was thoroughly gone into, with the final verdict falling that the word Pentecostal must stay. All these years they had been known as Pentecostals, with most of the Oneness organizations they had been associated with identifying themselves with that particular name. The Pentecostal Assemblies of the World, The Pentecostal Ministerial

Alliance, The Pentecostal Assemblies of Jesus Christ and The Pentecostal Church Incorporated had all used this name, and propagated it far and wide.

Then someone mentioned the word "United." All that they were endeavoring to accomplish was wrapped up in the one word, and it began getting a hold on each of them. Suddenly Hite stood, and tremblingly began to speak. He was overcome with emotion. Sitting here these hours, deliberating upon such a noble work, and now this word "United" injected at such an opportune time! He could not keep the tears back, and with tear-glistened cheek, his large arm slowly rising and falling, over and over he repeated this magical word, "United! United! United!"

As one man, all those in the room caught the spirit of this oration, and soon all were humbled by the feeling of a united Pentecostal church. Openly there was weeping, for all knew they probably were participating in one of the most important moments of their lives.

There was no question now about any of the deliberations of the past few hours and various meetings prior to this. A united Pentecostal church it must be, and what could be a grander name than that. It was then decided that they would recommend the new organization to be called the United Pentecostal Church. This name was destined to be carried into the far reaches of the earth.

THE MERGER

The General Conferences of the two organizations were to meet simultaneously in St. Louis, the latter part of September, 1945. They were to convene in separate locations to ratify the terms of the merger, and then come together for their first sessions as a united body.

In the meantime, a committee was appointed to harmonize the Manual. They were to prepare this agreement of the Articles of Faith and Constitution to be presented at these conventions for ratification. Those chosen from the PCI were Goss and Vouga, and those on this committee from the PAJC were Fauss and Ermin Bradley. These men worked seriously on this most important aspect of this genesis of harmony between these two churches. Finally they were ready to read the fruit of these hours of work.

Pastor Guinn's church was again the site of the PAJC conference. The PCI was to meet in the spacious Kiel Auditorium. Then, when both churches ratified the merger, they were to come together for their first joint sessions in this auditorium.

Coming together in the same confines of the last General Conference, the PAJC tackled the task before them. Soon, after hearing all the recommended propositions of the merger, they voted to ratify all the terms, and made preparation to move to the site of the initial meeting of the United Pentecostal Church.

Down in Kiel Auditorium anticipation was running high also. The PCI felt a little lost in the vastness of this large building, but knew that if all went well, the new organization would shortly be filling to capacity and overflowing this hall, and others similar to it across the nation from year to year.

All did go well, as they too ratified all the terms

of the merger, and now awaited the coming of the others of their newly-organized church. Thus the birth of the United Pentecostal Church came to pass.

THE FIRST MEETING
OF THE UNITED PENTECOSTAL CHURCH

The first gathering of this new church was held September 25, 1945. Brethren who had prayed desperately for such a union now rejoiced as they greeted one another. Tears were openly seen as men fell upon each other's shoulders, weeping with joy at their newly-found fellowship, and considering the prospects of the future. They were wise enough to know that many problems of adjustment would arise, but knew also that the strength derived from coming together would override any such disappointments. A sense of profound anticipation was felt throughout the united meeting.

"The first business session of the merged organization was held on Tuesday, September 25, 1945."[6] This was to be the election of officers, and it was natural that each mind was questioning itself on who these would be. "The following were elected: Howard A. Goss, General Superintendent; W. T. Witherspoon, Assistant General Superintendent; Stanley W. Chambers, General Secretary-Treasurer; T. R. Dungan, Assistant General Secretary-Treasurer; and Wynn T. Stairs, Foreign Missionary Secretary."[7]

The conference lasted two days after the merger, and was a definite success, with almost all feeling new energy to take back to their respective places of labor. There were, by this merger, approximately

1,800 ministers and 900 churches combined for biblical Oneness propagation. This was to grow considerably in the two decades that brings its history to the present moment.

[1]Private interview with O.F. Fauss, April 9, 1964.
[2]Ibid.
[3]William Ralph Inge, "New Dictionary of Thoughts," p. 728.
[4]Manual, United Pentecostal Church, 1964, p. 19.
[5]Proverbs 22:1
[6]Letter from S. W. Chambers, General Secretary-Treasurer, United Pentecostal Church.
[7]Ibid.

First General Board of the United Pentecostal Church

Chapter 16

The United Pentecostal
Church on the Move

With the union of the Pentecostal Church
Incorporated and the Pentecostal Assemblies of Jesus
Christ, a united effort in various fields of labor was
immediately inaugurated. Gradually momentum was accelerated to propel the cherished message as it never had
been done since the first century. The United Pentecostal
Church suddenly became a strong striking force to present the true Bible doctrinal position to the world.

There is nothing so forceful as combined effort
toward an intended goal. Senancour said, "Union does
everything when it is perfect. It satisfies desires, sim-
plifies needs, foresees the wishes, and becomes a constant fortune."[1] The Bible says, "Behold, how good and
how pleasant it is for brethren to dwell together in
unity!"[2]

A General organization has developed over the
years which has brought tremendous gains to the
overall work of the United Pentecostal Church.

THE GENERAL HEADQUARTERS
The General Headquarters of the United Pentecostal
Church was located from the beginning in St. Louis,
Missouri. The first Headquarters building was located

at 3449 South Grand Blvd. It was moved in 1952 to 3645 South Grand Blvd. where it remained until 1970 when a completely new building was erected at 8855 Dunn Road in Hazelwood, Missouri.

The staff in St. Louis is headed by the General Superintendent. Howard A. Goss was elected General Superintendent at the 1945 merger and held that office until the General Conference of 1951, when Arthur T. Morgan, who for several years pastored Faith Tabernacle in Port Arthur, Texas and was the Secretary-Treasurer of the Texas District, was elected to the General Superintendency.

All General Officers of the United Pentecostal Church are elected every two years, and Morgan had subsequently been elected since that time. Morgan served until his death in 1967. Stanley W. Chambers was elected in his place and served until 1977. At his retirement, Nathaniel A. Urshan was chosen to serve.

Chambers was first elected as General Secretary-Treasurer in 1945, and served until his elevation to the General Superintendent's office in 1967. Cleveland M. Becton was chosen in his place. Robert Lester McFarland was elected after Becton's resignation in 1976 and served until 1981 when he resigned. Cleveland M. Becton was again elected as General Secretary-Treasurer.

The United Pentecostal Church is governed between General Conferences by the General Board or Board of General Presbyters consisting of the General Superintendent, the Assistant General Superintendents, the General Secretary-Treasurer, the Director of Foreign Missions, the Director of Home Missions, the Editor of the Pentecostal Herald, and one General Presbyter from each organized district (the District Superintendent), the Director of Sunday School, and six Regional Executive Presbyters.

Between session of the Board of General Presbyters, the Executive Board takes the oversight of all business matters. This board consists of the General Superintendent; the two Assistant General Superintendents; the General Secretary, the Director of Home Missions; the Director of Foreign Missions, and the six Regional Executive Presbyters, plus one Canadian representative and an Eastern Zone District Superintendent and a Western Zone District Superintendent.

THE PENTECOSTAL PUBLISHING HOUSE

The United Pentecostal Church maintains a publishing plant in the St. Louis Headquarters, known as the Pentecostal Publishing House. It has proved to be an immense asset through the publishing of Sunday School literature, books and tracts, beside being a well-run bookstore. It has made an invaluable contribution to the propagation of the gospel, as Sunday Schools around the world are supplied with Oneness Sunday School material.

The first manager was T. R. Dungan, who was followed by J. O. Wallace in 1951. Wallace, in turn, was succeeded by Ray Agnew in 1953. David Schroeder followed Agnew in 1972 with Wallace again becoming General Manager in 1980. Through the years much expansion has been made to keep up with the demands of the fast-growing Oneness movement.

PUBLICATIONS

Besides Sunday School literature, tracts and books, the United Pentecostal Church Divisions each publish periodicals concerning their varied areas of labor.

Oneness circles have been blessed through the years with fine publications.

The Pentecostal Herald has proven a binding force through the years by keeping the United Pentecostal constituency informed of the many related happenings around the world. It has carried news of church activity and also vital articles concerned with both the doctrine and Christian living aspects of Oneness interest. The first editor was M. J. Wolff, who was appointed in 1945, and served until 1946, when he was succeeded by Paul H. Box. Upon his resignation in 1951, Lester R. Thompson became editor. When he resigned in 1955, Arthur L. Clanton was appointed editor. When Clanton died in 1976, Calvin L. Rigdon became editor. When he resigned in 1981, J. L. Hall was appointed editor.

THE GENERAL CONFERENCE

Each year in the early fall, there is a much-looked-for convention for the United Pentecostal Church. It is called The General Conference. From around the world people come to this annual church meeting, expecting to receive an inspiration that will send them back to their various places of labor with new hope and vision. Many feel a year would not be complete without attending this convention.

The General Conference deals with almost every facet of Pentecostal life, and for that reason it reaches almost everyone, whatever their particular interest in the work of the Lord. From the beginning of the opening prayer, until the last amen, much business is taken care of to project the largest Oneness church into another year of work in the interest of lost humanity.

The different departments: Foreign Missions, Home Missions, Harvestime Broadcast, Youth, Sunday School, Ladies Auxiliary and Bible Schools, each has its part, sharing with all in attendance its burden in the Lord's work.

Looking back, you cannot forget Memphis, Columbus, Kansas City, Dallas, St. Louis, Indianapolis, Little Rock, Tulsa, Duluth, Long Beach, San Antonio, New Orleans, Grand Rapids, Atlantic City, Portland, Miami, Houston, Salt Lake City, Louisville, Fort Worth, Anaheim, Indianapolis, Philadelphia, and other cities that have felt the surge of several thousand Pentecostals walking through their streets, eating in their restaurants and staying in their hotels.

Fellowship has always meant much to Pentecostals. Being a minority group, it is always a nice feeling to go where there are many others believing and feeling concerning the Scriptures as you do. This has always been another thrill Pentecostals have gotten from General Conference. Wonderful fellowship with those of like precious faith is enjoyed there.

THE DISTRICTS

The United Pentecostal Church constituency is divided into districts, usually separate states or a combination of states. There were 18 districts after the merger in 1945, and this has grown to 47.

Each district has a Superintendent and a Secretary-Treasurer who are elected for two year terms by the District Conference. The district is sometimes divided into sections, with each Sectional Conference electing a Sectional Presbyter and Sectional Secretary-Treasurer for one-year terms.

Each of the General Departments is organized accordingly throughout the districts. This is where the real strength of the United Pentecostal Church lies—the organizational structure from the Headquarters office down through the districts right into sections and on into the local church groups. Each district, each section and local church, though, is sovereign, so long as it works within the framework of the by-laws of the general organization. This lends impetus to the work, because when people are free to become "captains of their own ships," without anyone being able to interfere, they will usually feel led to accomplish more. They can make of it what they will, and this adds challenge.

FOREIGN MISSIONS

In the Gospel of Mark, chapter 16, Jesus said, "Go ye into all the world, and preach the gospel. . . ." In Acts, chapter 1, He said again, "But ye shall receive power, after the Holy Ghost is come upon you: and ye shall be witnesses unto me both in Jerusalem, and in Judea, and in Samaria, and unto the uttermost part of the earth."

This has been the heartbeat of the gospel since Christ first commissioned the church. The first-century church was replete with it. It was the very core which their lives revolved around. Uppermost in their thinking was that watchword of their Lord, "This gospel . . . shall be preached in all the world for a witness unto all nations. . . ."[3] And into their world they went, preaching everywhere, ". . .the Lord working with them, and confirming the word with signs following."[4] It was not too many years until all over the civilized world there was talk of the Christian church.

This, too, must be the motivating force of the church of this century. It is heart warming to know that one of the main reasons for organizing the church in the earlier part of the twentieth century was for missionary purposes.[5] That has also been one of the fundamental ideas through the years.

The Foreign Missionary Department is one of the most important bodies within the United Pentecostal Church. Much thinking revolves around missionary work, and many members of local churches devote much time to prayer and raising money for foreign missionaries.

The Director of Foreign Missions was known as the Foreign Missionary Secretary at the merger in 1945. Wynn T. Stairs, with his great burden and insight, was elected to this position. He served until 1962, when Oscar Vouga assumed the responsibility. Vouga, who for a number of years was an Assistant General Superintendent, was a former missionary to Hawaii, and brought wide experience and vision to this important place. Paul H. Box served from January, 1956 to December 31, 1975 as Foreign Missionary Secretary. In 1969 Tom Fred Tenney was elected and served until 1976. At this time Harry Scism became the director.

The department has grown through the years, with missionaries today in many countries in the world. There is a definite move throughout the church to see this number multiplied, and, with time, if the Lord tarries, this should be realized.

The department is under the direction of the Foreign Missionary Board, comprised of the Director, the Secretary, the Director of Promotion. and seven members from across the United States and Canada.

HOME MISSIONS

What was said in the beginning of the Foreign Missions section could also be said at the beginning of this one. "Into all the world" was the command. This means the next town or city, the next county, the next state also. The stronger the home front, the stronger the foreign—this is the thinking of the Home Missionary Department.

Many parts of America yet lie as a vast mission field to the Oneness message, and gradually penetrations are being made into several of these areas. Men and women with a pioneering spirit are shouldering this responsibility. The Home Missionary Department is doing much to inspire this giant effort, through its support of home missionaries, and with grants to purchase property and build new buildings.

There has also been concentrated efforts in some localities with the establishment of several churches where the Oneness Message had never been preached before.

The Home Missionary Department was inaugurated in 1952, with Stanley R. Hanby becoming its first

Director. George L. Glass Sr. followed Hanby in 1957, and he was, in turn, followed by C. Haskel Yadon in 1958. In 1967 J. T. Pugh became Director, and he was followed by V. Arlen Guidroz in 1973. He was succeeded by J. E. Yonts in 1976.

THE PENTECOSTAL CONQUERORS

The United Pentecostal Church is not failing to use the vigorous energy of its youth. Recognizing the vast accomplishment of youthful endeavor, much has been done in this quarter to convince Pentecostal young people that they have their place in the church.

One of the best known projects in the United Pentecostal Church is a youth endeavor—"Sheaves for Christ." This is the international youth mission program with the purpose of allowing youth to share in the great commission, "Go ye into all the world." It is a project of raising funds to help in carrying the gospel to the world. It is not only a fund-raising project, but a program designed to unite youth in a great world-wide effort, focusing their attention on the evangelization of the world.[6]

The Conquerors ages are 12 through 35. Most United Pentecostal Churches have a service each week for this group.

David F. Gray was the first President, being elected in 1946. Upon his resignation, Richard S. Davis was appointed to the office in 1948. He was followed by J. O. Moore in 1949, who continued until 1951. Calvin L. Rigdon was elected that year. It was under his leadership in 1952 that "Sheaves for Christ" came into being. He served until 1960, when the President Tom

Fred Tenney was elected. Kenneth Haney followed him in 1969. He served until 1971, when Donald Deck was appointed. Dan L. Rigdon became President in 1977. C. Patton Williams followed him in 1979. When Williams resigned in 1982, Rex D. Johnson was elected.

THE MISSIONS-YOUTH CONVENTION

Under the guidance of the Foreign Missionary Department, Home Missionary Department, and the Pentecostal Conquerors Department, a significant convention was started in 1961. It has developed into one of the outstanding gatherings in the United Pentecostal Church. The three departments have various times for their services, with the afternoons devoted to three workshops involving the three groups. It offers a tremendous opportunity for youth to become acquainted with the mission program.

THE SUNDAY SCHOOL

Pentecostalism, in some respects, has gone through a great change in the last few years. It has been realized that most converts are coming into the church initially through the Sunday School effort. Attracted through a visitation program, becoming interested through sound teaching, during the revival or in a regular Sunday service they pray through to the Pentecostal experience.

This has brought a new enthusiasm to Sunday School work. A new meaning has evolved from this knowledge. Not only can Sunday School be considered a teaching area of the church but it is a gigantic arm of evangelism.

Through the concerted efforts of churches across America in Sunday School efforts, the United Pentecostal Church is recognized as one of the fastest growing churches in the nation.

The first General Sunday School Director, E. E. McNatt, was elected in 1949. He was succeeded by J. O. Wallace in 1958 who served until 1974. Calvin A. Rigdon served from 1974 to 1976. James Boatman followed him in 1976. When Boatman resigned in 1982, E. J. McClintock was elected as Sunday School Director.

THE LADIES AUXILIARY

In this history of the Oneness movement, special recognition must be given the gallant women who have so nobly labored, no matter the consequences. Thriving churches of this hour would not exist if loyal, God-fearing women had not kept the doors open in years gone by. Courageous women have stood stalwartly by the side of their preacher husbands, bringing in new works or trying to carry on the old church. These women have taken our message to the mission fields, some being buried there. What can you say when a history is so replete with instances such as these?

The Ladies Auxiliary of the United Pentecostal Church is one of its unsung heroes. How many churches have had the church note paid by this group? The piano, organ, the carpet on the floor, pews, and various other things have been purchased by the sacrificial work of these soldiers of the cross.

The Ladies Auxiliary was actually in existence for

years but became an official department of the United Pentecostal Church in 1953, with Mary Cole becoming the first President. Under her leadership, the Mother's Memorial project came into being. This is a fundraising project for Home and Foreign Missions, besides helping greatly the Tupelo Children's Mansion, the United Pentecostal Church home for homeless children. She was succeeded in office by the late Ila Ashcraft in 1960. After her death in 1963, Vera Kinzie became President.

HARVESTIME® BROADCAST

It was Saturday night at the 1960 General Conference in Dallas. For many, a dream was coming true, as the first thirty-minute radio broadcast was taped before the assembled conference. Shouts were heard from the thousands in the congregation as the Harvestime choir sang the opening chorus and then as the booming voice of the announcer, J. Hugh Rose, said, "This is Harvestime, the radio voice of the United Pentecostal Church." Then came the stirring message of the speaker, Nathaniel A. Urshan, and more shouts were heard.

For years a national broadcast had been the desire of many of the ministers, and in 1959 a committee of exploration had been appointed to go ahead with the project. The broadcast in the Dallas conference was the fruit of this exhaustive study, and plans were made to begin the actual broadcast to the nation on the first Sunday of March, 1961.

It was learned soon that more than a shout was needed to keep a broadcast of this stature on the air.

It took money and lots of it, but steadily the program has taken hold and the number of stations has increased. Harvestime is a well-planned and operated program, and can be heard each Sunday across the nation. The faithful personnel directly involved deserves commendation for their unceasing work in this medium of gospel propagation.

The broadcast is under the guidance of the Harvestime Radio Commission.

[1]The New Dictionary of Thoughts, p. 696.
[2]Psalm 133:1.
[3]Matthew 24:14.
[4]Mark 16:20.
[5]S. C. McClain, "Notes," The Move of God, p. 5, 6.
[6]Manual, United Pentecostal Church, 1964, p. 70, 71.

1955 General Board of the United Pentecostal Church

Chapter 17

Four Vital Elements

There are four very important factors in the life of the United Pentecostal Church, which we will deal with in this chapter. These are camp meetings, youth camps, Bible colleges and the Tupelo Children's Mansion.

CAMP MEETINGS

The summer camp meeting to many is the highlight of the year. Great care is taken to be able to attend these annual events where hundreds, and, in several places, thousands, will come together to hear good, down-to-earth, solid Bible teaching, fiery evangelistic messages, well-trained choirs singing the old and often times new hymns, and other vocalists singing praises of, and to, the Lord Jesus Christ.

Anyone will admit, who has ever been caught up in its spirit, that there just isn't anything like camp meeting. Though it will be hot and dusty, the lines getting into the dining hall will be long, the benches are certainly not comfortable as the pews back in the home church, but there's something about the camp meeting atmosphere that causes people to forget, or possibly endure, all this for the blessing of spiritual teaching, the inspiration of sacred worship and the invigorating fellowship of getting together with old friends and God's people.

This has been the story, year after year, for Oneness people, and they have had rich and rewarding experience with these meetings.

"Camp meetings served several good purposes. Not only was there an opportunity for saints and ministers to get together and become acquainted in a special fellowship, but also for teaching the great truths of the Bible. In these Bible studies many have been convinced of the message of reconciliation, 'To wit, that God was in Christ, reconciling the world unto himself.'[1] In a camp meeting at Hot Springs, Arkansas, where the writer was a sponsor with the late H. E. Reed, we baptized fifty in the mighty name of Jesus, of which thirty-five received the Holy Ghost and spoke in tongues either in the water or while still near the baptistry, including three ministers (two Methodists and one Baptist)."[2]

Practically all the districts have camp meeting each summer and most own their own campgrounds. The size of the district determines the size of the tabernacle. They run from smaller ones, seating a few hundred, to large buildings seating several thousand. Most camps have a day children's church, and a youth service while the adult service is in progress.

It is a marked certainty that many church groups who at one time had camp meetings, but who no longer have members interested in such, have lost their evangelistic fervor and love for worship and the

Word of God. Pentecostals feel that if the day arrives for them when they no longer desire what camp meetings provide then something will be vastly missing in their Christian experience.

YOUTH CAMPS

"I have been around Pentecost a long time, and I personally feel that in the hour we live the greatest single contribution to the church is what our youth camps are doing." An elderly minister recently made this statement, and numbers would heartily agree with him.

Youth Camps are comparatively new in the United Pentecostal Church, coming into existence in the early 1950's. About then it was more and more realized that something had to be done about the great loss to the church of the countless young people across the nation. The teens seemed to be the most vulnerable age in Pentecostal society, so something had to be done. It was at this time that Sheaves for Christ[3] was introduced through the Youth Department.

District leaders began searching for something that would add great spiritual depth and love for the truth to the experience of the young, and Youth Camps seemed to be the answer. They were small in attendance at first, with a handful of instructors (the author remembers one such when he was asked to be the only instructor besides the camp evangelist), but they caught fire quickly, until now thousands of young people are in attendance every summer. It takes countless administrative personnel to get the job done, but all can see the great benefit this endeavor has been.

Every summer hundreds receive the baptism of the Holy Spirit and many are baptized in water in these camps. New inspiration is derived to live for the Lord, no matter the price. Acquaintances made across the district mean a great deal to the campers, and add greater desire to live for God so that they won't disappoint these new friends.

From early in the morning until the middle of the afternoon the campers go from class to class, garnering many things from the Word of the Lord taught by capable teachers. The recreational period follows, which is usually enjoyed by the administrative personnel as much as by the young people themselves. Then at night there is a giant evangelistic service, with a speaker of note preaching on a level where youth can understand. The altars are usually filled at the conclusion of the service, and here these campers learn to pray as never before, when they travail for the hungry young hearts who are seeking to be filled with the Spirit.

Many things happen in a week's time to encourage faith in a young person's life. A humorous incident that speaks of a young thirteen-year-old-boy's heart after living in such an atmosphere for a week, was overheard by the Texas District Pentecostal Conquerors President, Jack DeHart. Two boys were discussing the fact they were out of money, with only a dime apiece, and were wondering what they would do to get to their homes. One of them spoke up and said, "Well, let's go drink an R.C., and just trust God."

Much of this teaching has been carried over into every day at home and in school life, and has paid off immeasurably. The United Pentecostal Church is not losing nearly so many of its young people as before, and youth camp deserves much of the credit.

BIBLE COLLEGES

Tryon Edwards said, "Early instruction in truth will best keep out error." Someone has well said, "Fill the bushel with wheat, and you may defy the Devil to fill it with tares." Through thinking such as this in Christian Education, the machinery of the church will be oiled with truth for a long time.

Bible Colleges have certainly had their place in the United Pentecostal Church. Their contribution has been considerably more than most would probably imagine. On close observation, it is seen that a great number of the ministers have received training in Bible School. Those who have had this opportunity are usually very outspoken in favor of this type of training. They know more than anyone else where they would probably be without the tremendous help the hours of study gave them.

Because of the great expense in operating a college, the United Pentecostal Church Bible schools have had a struggle through the years. Yet their presence is keenly felt throughout the fellowship, with many former students pastoring churches and holding varied district offices.

Bible colleges have had their place since the early days of the century, with the initial twentieth century outpouring of the Holy Ghost in the Bethel Bible School in Topeka, Kansas. "In the early days of Pentecost, great leaders began having short-term faith

Bible schools, where young ministers would be taught the Word of God, the art of soulwinning, and how to trust God for all their needs in the gospel work. These schools usually ran from 30 to 90 days. Daniel C. O. Opperman, a college professor of San Antonio, Texas, came into the faith and began each late winter to hold 30 to 60 days of school.

"In the autumn of 1916, Mother Barnes and Brother and Sister Opperman purchased a large 61-room health resort hotel in Eureka Springs, Arkansas and arranged for a faith Bible school called Ozark Bible and Literary School, with several consecrated teachers. They all lived by faith, trusting God to miraculously supply every need. Not a teacher had a promise of compensation for his services, there was no charge for tuition, and old and young alike came to study the Word. Several families moved to Eureka Springs to put their children in literary schools which had grades through the ninth.

"On January 1, 1918 the writer joined the faculty and taught the eighth grade, which gave us several young prospects for the ministry. Some of these have preached for years this wonderful Oneness Jesus' name message. They include C. P. and Mary Williams of Tulsa, Oklahoma, along with Albert and Odel Cagle of California."[4]

Those beginnings helped some to recognize the tremendous value a systematic study course could be to the minister and Christian worker. In the thirties and forties those pioneering in this field, which had a tremendous impact upon the Oneness movement, through training many of its ministers and lay workers, were S. G. Norris, C. P. Williams, L. W. Coote, C. D. Soper, E. Rohn, L. C. Reed and A. D. Hurt.

The United Pentecostal Church now finds itself blessed with several Bible Colleges: Apostolic Bible Institute, St. Paul, Minnesota; Gateway College of Evangelism, St. Louis, Missouri; Jackson College of Ministries, Jackson, Mississippi; Texas Bible College, Houston, Texas; Christian Life College, Stockton, California; Kent Christian College, Dover, Delaware; United Pentecostal Bible Institute, Fredericton, New Brunswick, Canada; Apostolic Missionary Institute, London, Ontario, Canada; and Indiana Bible College, Seymour, Indiana.

Overseeing the Bible College work, according to the general educational policy of the United Pentecostal Church, is the Board of Christian Education. An annual inspection of each school is made by members of this board.

TUPELO CHILDREN'S MANSION

The author was sitting in a Bible College chapel service enthralled by the earnest appeal being made from the pulpit. Tears glistened on the cheeks of the speaker as he told of the heavy burden on his heart to see a Oneness Pentecostal home for homeless children. Seeing many instances where Pentecostal children, after some tragic happening, had to be taken in by other church groups, he lamented the cold fact that the United Pentecostal Church had no such place to take care of its own homeless children. The man speaking so forcefully was T. C. Montgomery.

From that meeting for a number of years he traveled thousands of miles through several states, making the same appeal, and raising funds to establish such an institution. Churches and Districts rallied to the call, and in the late fall of 1953 the doors of beautiful new facilities swung open to receive its first inhabitants, precious children to be reared in a wonderfully spiritual atmosphere.

Montgomery's dream became a reality, and in Tupelo, Mississippi on a beautiful hillside is the lovely campus of Tupelo Children's Mansion.

L. J. Hosch was the first Superintendent, and after two years he was followed by R. P. Kloepper. B. Brian Chelette followed him in 1971. He was succeeded by Stephen Drury in 1976.

The Mansion is a well organized effort, with a Board of Directors from the many Districts supporting it, and an Executive Board from the Board of Directors.

Funds have been channeled to the mansion from individual donors, churches, districts, The Ladies Auxiliary[5] and The Pentecostal Conquerors.[6]

[1]II Corinthians 5:18, 19
[2]McClain, "Notes," p. 32, 33.
[3]Manual, United Pentecostal Church, 1964, p. 70, 71.
[4]McClain, "Notes," p. 18-30, 31.
[5]Page 145.
[6]Page 143.

Arthur T. Morgan

A. T. Morgan served as General Superintendent of the United Pentecostal Church from 1951 until his death in 1967.

S. W. Chambers

S. W. Chambers served as General Secretary-Treasurer from 1945 until 1967 when he was elected General Superintendent. He resigned in 1977.

Chapter 18

Second Generation Leadership

The 1967 United Pentecostal Church General Conference, in Tulsa, Oklahoma, became a moment of great change. Arthur T. Morgan, the General Superintendent for the last sixteen years, suddenly died while conducting a meeting of the general board. With this death began the second generation rise to take the leadership role of 20th century Pentecostalism. It is unique at this writing, that the church of this century, has in each area of the general leadership, a person who is a second generation Pentecostal, or of contemporary age.

Later in the conference Stanley W. Chambers was elected to succeed Morgan as General Superintendent, and became the first second generation General Superintendent. As a very young man, Chambers was elected to the office of General Secretary at the merger conference in 1945, and then served as a second generation Pentecostal through 22 years. He would now lead the way in the top leadership position of the UPC.

Chambers' father, George C. Chambers, has been a long time preacher and pastor. Young Chambers grew up in a preacher's home, when his father was an assistant pastor to the first assistant General Superintendent W. C. Witherspoon. His father later became pastor of the Columbus, Ohio church when Witherspoon passed away.

At the time of Morgan's death the two assistant general superintendents were also pioneer preachers of the 20th century Pentecostals. They were Oliver F. Fauss and Ralph G. Cook. In 1973 Fauss retired at the age of 73 and James L. Kilgore was elected in that position. In 1971 Cook retired at the age of 72. Nathaniel A. Urshan was elected to fill the position. Both of these newly elected officials are second generation Pentecostals.

Kilgore's father was a pioneer preacher who founded a number of churches in the southwest. Kilgore learned the sacrifice of the pioneer preacher's family during the depression years of the thirties, as his preacher father moved the family from one home mission work to another.

Urshan grew up in a Pentecostal preacher's home. His father A. D. Urshan, immigrated to the United States from Persia as a young man. He became a missionary, evangelist, and pastor, and young Urshan was given much valuable experience.

Cleveland M. Becton became the second of the second generation to assume leadership. When Chambers was elevated to the general superintendency in 1967 Becton was elected in his place as General Secretary. Becton did not grow up in a preacher's home, but he had a preacher uncle he was close to. His uncle was G. H. Brown, longtime Little Rock, Arkansas pastor, in whose church he received the Holy

Ghost. From Brown's pastoral leadership, as well as his own godly home, he learned the principles of the pioneers. He served as General Secretary until 1976, when he resigned to pastor in Nashville, Tennessee.

At this time Robert Lester McFarland, the District Superintendent of Indiana was elected in Becton's place. McFarland also, is a second generation Pentecostal. McFarland's father was for many years a pastor in Indiana, so McFarland had much opportunity to garner great insight into what 20th century pentecostalism was all about. McFarland served as General Secretary until 1981 when he resigned to accept appointment as Regional Field Supervisor of Europe/Middle East, Foreign Missions Division.

In 1977, Chambers retired from the office of General Superintendent, and Urshan was elected to take his place. In this conference Becton was elected to serve in Urshan's place as Assistant General Superintendent. He served until 1981 when he was again elected as General Secretary-Treasurer. At this time Jesse F. Williams, District Superintendent of North Carolina, was elected as Assistant General Superintendent.

Since 1973 the United Pentecostal Church has had second generation leadership in each of the four top positions. This is an important observation, as history has pungently said that weakening change can come with succeeding generations. We trust this historical observation will not be the plight of the United Pentecostal Church, and have high hopes that this church will continue its strong evangelistic thrust into the latter part of the 20th century.

1980 General Board of the United Pentecostal Church

Chapter 19

Where To From Here

Revival must not die! It must not cease to spread. Pentecost must continue its history of evangelization. Its saving and teaching zeal must still be uppermost in its thinking. Its drive and motivation must continue to come from the vast need of the lost millions around the world.

History is quick to point its finger at other church groups founded upon noble ideals and then becoming self-satisfied and at ease in Zion after some successes. In this chapter we set forth certain practical "musts" for the future of the Oneness movement and, in particular, the United Pentecostal Church, if she wills to survive the tragic fate of others.

REVIVAL MUST NOT DIE

The term *revival* when associated with religion means "a period of religious awakening, or renewed interest in religion after indifference and decline."[1] It also means "an awakening in a church or community of interest in, and care for, matters of personal religion."[2]

The spirit that causes this must continue. The burden, compassion, feeling, and urgency which bring this to pass in an individual's heart, must live on. Great sacrifice has brought the truths expressed in this book to the present time. This must persist.

History tells us that true scriptural revival fires have been fanned into existence through man's facing up to his personal responsibility to God. The Oneness movement must continue to bring man face to face with this solemn duty.

Anointed evangelistic preaching, fervent altar appeals and heart-warming altar services must be, as in the past, the order in our modern age.

Some have said, "The day of revival is over," but this is not true. Wherever honest, scriptural and dedicated effort is being made to have revival, God is blessing in this hour. This does not necessarily mean that large numbers will come in (on the contrary, it may mean just a few), but gradually churches are growing, with new people taking their places in the congregation; older saints are encouraged to press the battle on, and morale, as a whole, is high.

But the price for revival must be paid today, and, as always, it involves a determined dedication to the following:

(1) **Prayer**—Prayer must be an integral part in the life of the individual Christian and the complete church. We will do well in keeping prayer a vital element in the Oneness movement.

(2) **Fasting**—Jesus said, "This kind goeth not out but by prayer and fasting,"[3] teaching us that some things can only be accomplished through

—181—

such desperate action.

(3) **Faithfulness**—Church attendance, tithing, offerings and other numerous things are done only by faithful people. God blesses a people who will sincerely pursue them.

(4) **Personal Work**—Slowly the Oneness movement is recapturing this vision. One of the things they said about the early twentieth century Pentecostals was, "Everyone of them is a preacher." This wasn't true, of course, but all testified of their experience everywhere they went, endeavoring to bring others into this glorious experience.

In some quarters it is suspected that some are just trying to hold their own, harboring the pessimistic idea that no one is going to come in anyway. Let us not be deceived. This kind of attitude will rock us to sleep, and the movement will become as others.

We "must" persist in a strong evangelistic effort.

SUNDAY SCHOOL—A VITAL PART
OF EVANGELISM AND EDUCATION

Sunday School has taken on new meaning for Oneness thinking in the last several years. The Oneness movement is recognizing clearly the vast potential in reaching souls through the Sunday School department.

In a changing world it is true that we have a changeless gospel, but effective methods must be wisely adhered to in order to get those outside the church to hear the same gospel the early church preached.

Gradually we Pentecostals are finding out how a well co-ordinated Sunday School effort can attract the outsiders into the church, and how much easier it gets the work of the church: evangelization and indoctrination, accomplished.

A well-organized systematic Sunday School is a must to the future Oneness movement because it does three things: first, evangelization; second, indoctrination; and third, it offers many avenues of service in these two fields to the individual church member.

Combining avenues of service with the two first mentioned, let us see the terrific push it gives to the propagation of the gospel message.

(1) "**Evangelization**"—Jesus commanded the church, "Go ye into all the world, and preach the gospel to every creature."[4] He also stated the tremendous task of the church when He said, "Ye shall receive power, after that the Holy Ghost is come upon you: and ye shall be witnesses unto me."[5]

We see by this that the main and predominant work the church must be devoted to is evangelizing the world. This must permeate the very air we breathe, and never should we lose consciousness of it. That is where the Sunday School comes in.

The Sunday School offers a wonderful medium in getting this tremendous job completed.

Sunday School drives had been the mode in most churches for a long time. The number was run up for a few Sundays and then it would fall back down to normal again, with the chance of gaining a few. This helped morale for a while, but after the drive most quit working, waiting for the next drive.

Then the question came, "Why not have a Sunday School push all the time?" This seemed logical, but how best to keep the interest high and people working continually? It was deduced that this would come through an organized, active weekly visitation program. Sunday School administrative workers, teachers and members of classes could meet, to go door-to-door, seeking new ones and taking care of follow-up work on those who recently attended. Various methods have been devised. Conclusive proof has been offered that it works, and works wondrously, with many more being brought into this New Testament truth.

(2) "**Indoctrination**"—Jesus in the great commission said, "Go ye therefore, and teach all nations . . . teaching them to observe all things whatsoever I have commanded you. . . ."[6] We readily see that after we lead men to obey the gospel we must indoctrinate them in the things of God. Where is a better place than the Sunday School?

Most churches allow one hour and fifteen minutes for Sunday School, with the most time devoted to class work and study. This affords the church a fine opportunity to complete this essential task commanded by the Lord Himself. We must teach or perish! We must recognize that Sunday School is that great opening the church needs in this hour.

If Oneness Pentecostals do not indoctrinate the students in their Sunday School now, and in the future if the Lord tarries, the young generation will not appreciate the basic fundamental doctrines, and will be swallowed up in ecumenism.

In a recent test the author gave to 131 freshmen

Bible college students, he was shocked at the lack in knowledge of basic Oneness truths. The Pentecostal Conquerors tested students at several youth camps in a recent year, and found, to their amazement, that the basic truths were the least understood. The greater majority in these two tests had grown up in Pentecostal Sunday Schools.

This speaks loudly to us all. For years we have taken for granted that they were getting what they needed. As we are awakening to the fact that they were not, let us re-evaluate our teaching principles and rise up to meet this crucial challenge.

So, as the Oneness movement steers its ship unto the uncharted waters of the future, she *must* be profoundly Sunday School minded. She must recognize its invaluable contribution in putting the church to work doing the job Jesus commanded us to do. Usually the larger the Sunday School, the larger the revival crowds! The larger the revival crowds, the more the people who pray through to the Old Time Religion.

BIBLE COLLEGES MUST SHARE
THIS RESPONSIBILITY

Because the majority of the students presently attending our Bible Colleges are prospective ministers of the gospel, it is awesomely imperative that the schools share the burden of evangelization and indoctrination.

If the Lord tarries, some of the leaders of the future church are being taught in our colleges. Where will they take the church? What will they teach our children and grandchildren? This is extremely important to us all.

As the administration of each college ponders this type of thinking, it becomes a front-running job to make sure that each student spends many hours studying basic Pentecostal Doctrine. The Godhead, Baptism, Holy Ghost experience, and Holiness must be properly dealt with, and each student receive a clear understanding.

The contribution our Bible Colleges can make must not be underestimated. They can be our salvation or our ruination.

So another must is that Bible Colleges must challenge students to take the gospel into all the world, and at the same time indoctrinate them with sound teaching from the Word of God.

MISSIONS—A MUST

Foreign and Home Missions must be mentioned here in the light of the above. The eyes of the Oneness movement must continually be upon the harvest fields. Jesus admonished, "Say not ye, There are yet four months, and then cometh harvest? behold, I say unto you, Lift up your eyes, and look on the fields; for they are white already to harvest."[7]

We dare not forget our missionary endeavor. The missions spirit must envelop our activity, and continued effort be made. The challenge of this hour is to do better than we ever have. We must ever launch farther out into the deep of missionary accomplishment.

More prayer, sacrifice and finance is the future's crying need, to be able to send other devoted men and women to the mission field, both foreign and home.

On every hand it is believed that this is our hour,

this is our time, this is our opportunity, this is the chance we have waited for. Let us move out with accelerated speed to new horizons, and conquer new frontiers in this vast field.

LOSE NOT THE PIONEERING SPIRIT

The spirit of sacrifice that has established churches across the world must not be lost, for this is the spirit which has made Pentecost strong. Her bravery, and willingness to labor in the difficult places has made the march to victory progressive.

In the age of ease in which we live, this spirit will not be hard to lose. Our young people will have to be taught to be pioneers. The dying, hell-bound mass of humanity must be kept continually before them, along with the power of the gospel to save. If so, it is sure that such a great challenge will, with the call of God, cause them to reach for a more fulfilling work than the church has ever known.

God is calling more preachers, more than we have churches for them to preach in, so the answer must be that He is wanting churches to be established in the "next town"[8] "for a witness."[9] This will only come through a continued pioneering spirit.

[1]Webster's Dictionary.
[2]The New Century Dictionary.
[3]Matthew 17:21.
[4]Mark 16:15.
[5]Acts 1:8.
[6]Matthew 28:19, 20.
[7]John 4:35.
[8]Mark 1:38.
[9]Matthew 24:14.

Nathaniel A. Urshan

Nathaniel A. Urshan was elected as General Superintendent of the United Pentecostal Church in 1977. He has served as speaker for our international radio voice, *Harvestime*®, since its beginning in 1961.

Cleveland M. Becton

Cleveland M. Becton was elected as General Secretary-Treasurer in 1967 and served until he resigned in 1976. He was again elected as General Secretary-Treasurer in 1981.

James L. Kilgore

James L. Kilgore was elected as Assistant General Superintendent for the Western Zone of the United Pentecostal Church in 1973.

Jesse F. Williams

Jesse F. Williams was elected as Assistant General Superintendent for the Eastern Zone of the United Pentecostal Church in 1981.

First Headquarters of the United Pentecostal Church

Second Headquarters of the United Pentecostal Church

World Evangelism Center of the United Pentecostal Church

J. O. Wallace

J. O. Wallace was first appointed General Manager of the Pentecostal Publishing House in 1951 and served until his resignation in 1953. Later he served as Sunday School Director from 1958 until 1974. He was again appointed manager of the Publishing House in 1980.

R. L. McFarland

Robert L. McFarland was elected General Secretary-Treasurer of the United Pentecostal Church in 1976 and served until he resigned in 1981. He was then appointed Regional Field Director of Europe/Middle East with the Foreign Missions Division.